# LEGENDS OF VOLLEYBALL



50

## 50 Iconic Athletes and the Stories that Defined Them, for Young Readers

KIMMICH PRINTS

USA
QAT
CEV
9
Eczacıbaşı
13
CEV
HDI

# TABLE OF CONTENTS

# TABLE OF CONTENTS

# TABLE OF CONTENTS

TABLE OF CONTENTS



## Disclaimer

The stories and achievements of the athletes featured in "Legends of Volleyball: 50 Iconic Athletes and the Stories that Defined Them, for Young Readers" are based on publicly available information and sources. While every effort has been made to ensure accuracy and completeness, some details may vary, and interpretations of the athletes' careers and impacts are those of the author.

This book is intended for educational and inspirational purposes, aimed at young readers who are passionate about volleyball and sports in general. The inclusion of specific athletes does not imply endorsement or affiliation. Any errors or omissions are unintentional, and readers are encouraged to explore further and verify information through additional sources.

# INTRODUCTION

Welcome to "Legends of Volleyball: 50 Iconic Athletes and the Stories that Defined Them, for Young Readers." In the vibrant world of sports, few games captivate the imagination quite like volleyball. From the thunderous spikes to the graceful digs, each match tells a story of athleticism, teamwork, and sheer determination.

In this book, we'll journey through the captivating tales of 50 legendary athletes who have made an indelible mark on the sport. These aren't just stories of victories and defeats; they're narratives of passion, resilience, and triumph against the odds.
As young readers explore the lives of these remarkable individuals, they'll discover the power of perseverance, the joy of camaraderie, and the endless possibilities within the world of sports. From towering figures of the past to rising stars of today, each athlete's journey serves as inspiration for the next generation of volleyball enthusiasts.

Through captivating anecdotes, vivid imagery, and insightful commentary, "Legends of Volleyball" celebrates the rich mosaic of talent and tenacity that defines this beloved sport. Whether you're a seasoned player, an aspiring athlete, or simply a fan of the game, prepare to be inspired by the extraordinary feats and unforgettable stories within these pages.

Join us as we pay tribute to the heroes of volleyball, whose legacy continues to inspire and shape the future of the sport. This is their story. This is your invitation to greatness. Welcome to the world of "Legends of Volleyball."

Jordan Larson
(USA)

Jordan Quinn Larson is a decorated American volleyball player who has consistently delivered exceptional performances throughout her impressive career.

A DOMINANT FORCE ON THE COURT (1986-PRESENT):

- Born: October 16, 1986, Hooper, Nebraska, USA
- Height: 1.88 meters (6 feet 2 inches)
- Position: Outside Hitter (renowned for her powerful attacks and strategic game sense)

COLLEGE STARDOM (2006-2009):

- Played for Pennsylvania State University (Penn State) – a powerhouse program in collegiate volleyball.
- Won four consecutive National Collegiate Athletic Association (NCAA) championships (2007-2009) – a remarkable feat.
- Earned numerous individual accolades:

    - Big Ten Player of the Year (2006 & 2009)
    - First-team All-American (2006-2009)
    - NCAA Championship Most Outstanding Player (2007 & 2008)

NATIONAL TEAM SUCCESS (2009-PRESENT):

- A mainstay of the US Women's National Volleyball Team for over a decade.
- Secured a gold medal at the 2020 Tokyo Summer Olympics, solidifying her legacy.
- Won silver at the 2012 London Olympics and bronze at the 2016 Rio de Janeiro Olympics.
- Numerous medals at FIVB Volleyball World Cups, Nations Leagues, and other international tournaments.

PROFESSIONAL CAREER (2010-PRESENT):

- Played professionally for various clubs worldwide, showcasing her talent in:Italy
- Poland
- Azerbaijan
- China
- Most recently, Brazil (as of May 2024) with Minas Tênis Clube

PLAYING STYLE AND LEGACY:

- Renowned for her exceptional hitting power, impressive jumping ability, and strategic decision-making on the court.
- Considered one of the most consistent and reliable outside hitters of her generation.
- Her contributions have significantly impacted the US National Team's performance, inspiring future generations.
- A role model for young athletes, demonstrating dedication, work ethic, and perseverance.

Jordan Larson's exceptional talent, longevity at the top of the sport, and leadership qualities have solidified her place as an American volleyball legend. She continues to be an inspiration for aspiring athletes around the world.

# Karch Kiraly (USA)

EARLY LIFE AND INSPIRATION:

- Karch Kiraly was born in Jackson, Michigan in 1960.
- Growing up, he played many sports, but volleyball stole his heart after seeing a high school game.
- He was inspired by the teamwork, athleticism, and strategic thinking involved.

TRAINING AND DEDICATION:

- Karch practiced volleyball relentlessly, honing his skills in setting, hitting, and serving.
- He wasn't the tallest player, but he made up for it with incredible jumping ability and a strategic mind.
- He faced challenges early on, doubted by some because of his height, but used that as fuel to train even harder.

CAREER HIGHLIGHTS AND ACHIEVEMENTS:

- Karch achieved the seemingly impossible – becoming a legend in BOTH indoor and beach volleyball!
  - Indoor Volleyball:Led the USA Men's team to Olympic gold medals in 1984 and 1988, showcasing exceptional teamwork and leadership.
  - Won the World Championship in 1986, solidifying the USA's dominance in the sport.
  - Beach Volleyball:Pioneered the sport in its early days and became a global icon.
  - Won the very first Olympic gold medal in beach volleyball with teammate Kent Steffes in 1996, Atlanta.
  - Won a staggering 148 beach volleyball tournaments throughout his career.

IMPACT ON THE SPORT:

- Karch's success in both indoor and beach volleyball helped popularize the sport worldwide.

- He's considered one of the most intelligent and well-rounded volleyball players ever, inspiring countless athletes.
- After retiring as a player, Karch transitioned to coaching, leading the USA Women's team to their first-ever Olympic gold medal in 2020 (Tokyo Olympics).

BEYOND THE COURT:

- Karch is known for his friendly personality and passion for promoting volleyball at all levels.
- He enjoys surfing, spending time with his family, and inspiring young athletes.
- Fun Fact: Karch's nickname, "Karch," is actually a misspelling of his birth name, Charles.

INSPIRATIONAL QUOTE:

"The best teams are the ones that trust and respect each other the most. It's about having fun and enjoying the competition, but also understanding that you need to work hard together to win." - Karch Kiraly

# Lorenzo Bernardi (Italy)

EARLY LIFE AND INSPIRATION:

- Born in Trento, Italy in 1968, Lorenzo Bernardi wasn't always a powerhouse hitter.
- He started his volleyball journey as a setter, but his coaches saw his potential for more.
- With dedication and hard work, Lorenzo transformed into a dominant all-around player.

TRAINING AND DEDICATION:

- Known for his relentless work ethic, Lorenzo trained tirelessly to refine his skills in hitting, blocking, and serving.
- He wasn't afraid to push himself, becoming known for his powerful attacks and incredible leaping ability.
- Despite facing intense competition within the Italian team, Lorenzo used it as motivation to constantly improve.

CAREER HIGHLIGHTS AND ACHIEVEMENTS:

- Earning the nickname "The Czar" for his dominance on the court, Lorenzo led Italy to volleyball glory:Olympic Silver Medal: Though they didn't clinch the gold, Italy's silver medal win at the 1996 Atlanta Olympics was a significant achievement.
- Two-Time World Champion: Lorenzo led Italy to World Championship victories in 1990 and 1994, showcasing their strategic teamwork.
- Two-Time European Champion: Victories in 1989 and 1995 solidified Italy's position as a European volleyball powerhouse.
- Club Level Success: Lorenzo also achieved success at the club level, winning numerous championships with teams like Modena and Sisley Treviso.

IMPACT ON THE SPORT:

- Lorenzo's influence goes beyond his impressive trophy collection. His all-around skills and leadership inspired a generation of Italian volleyball players.

- He's considered one of the most complete volleyball players ever, excelling in every aspect of the game.
- After retiring from playing, Lorenzo transitioned to coaching, sharing his knowledge and passion for the sport with younger athletes.

BEYOND THE COURT:

- Lorenzo is known for his competitive spirit on the court, but also for his calm and collected demeanor off it.
- He enjoys spending time with his family, cycling, and giving back to the sport he loves.
- Fun Fact: Lorenzo's son, Riccardo Bernardi, has followed in his father's footsteps and is a professional volleyball player in Italy.

INSPIRATIONAL QUOTE:

"Volleyball is more than just hitting the ball. It's about teamwork, strategy, and pushing yourself to be the best you can be." - Lorenzo Bernardi

# Brenda Castillo (Dominican Republic)

Brenda Castillo is a phenomenal volleyball player from the Dominican Republic, renowned for her exceptional defensive skills and nicknamed "Chin Chin" (meaning "small portion" in Dominican slang) due to her height.

EARLY LIFE AND VOLLEYBALL BEGINNINGS (1992-PRESENT):

- Born: June 5, 1992, Bajos de Haina, Dominican Republic
- Height: 1.68 meters (5 ft 6 in)
- Married to Julio Enrique de los Santos.
- Began playing volleyball at the young age of 10 under the guidance of coach Valentín Arias Pérez in the club Siglo XXI.

A DEFENSIVE DYNAMO (2009-PRESENT):

- Plays the libero position, specializing in exceptional floor defense and receiving.
- Renowned for her quick reflexes, agility, and ability to read the opponent's attacks, earning her the nickname "La reina del patio" (The Queen of the Court) in Spanish.
- Her defensive prowess is instrumental in setting the pace for the Dominican Republic national team and various clubs she's played for.

NATIONAL TEAM SUCCESS (2010-PRESENT):

- A mainstay of the Dominican Republic Women's National Volleyball Team since 2010.
- Won a gold medal at the 2019 Pan American Games and the 2023 Central American and Caribbean Games, showcasing her defensive contributions to the team's success.
- Numerous other medals at Pan American Cups and other international tournaments.
- Known for her leadership qualities and positive energy on the court.

PROFESSIONAL CAREER (2010-PRESENT):

- Played for various clubs worldwide throughout her career, demonstrating her defensive skills in:
    - Dominican Republic
    - Azerbaijan
    - Brazil (most recently with Allianz Vero Volley Milano as of May, 2024)
- Her defensive contributions have been valuable assets to the teams she has played for.

Brenda Castillo's exceptional defensive skills, leadership, and positive attitude have solidified her place as a volleyball legend in the Dominican Republic and a respected athlete internationally. She continues to inspire aspiring players, particularly young girls, to excel in the sport.

# Sergey Tetyukhin (Russia)

EARLY LIFE AND INSPIRATION:

- Born in Fergana, Uzbekistan (then part of the USSR) in 1975, Sergey Tetyukhin's volleyball journey began under his father's guidance.
- At 16, he joined his first professional team, Krylya Vostoka Tashkent.
- A year later, with the collapse of the Soviet Union, his family moved to Belgorod, Russia, where his volleyball destiny unfolded.

TRAINING AND DEDICATION:

- Joining the Belogorie Belgorod club in 1992 turned out to be a defining moment.
- Sergey's dedication to training was legendary. He honed his skills as a powerful outside hitter, known for his exceptional jumping ability and precise aiming.
- He faced competition from talented teammates, but his perseverance and work ethic helped him stand out.

CAREER HIGHLIGHTS AND ACHIEVEMENTS:

- Sergey's career spanned an incredible 20 years with the Russian national team, a record few players can match:
    - Olympic Champion: He finally achieved Olympic gold at the 2012 London Games, after participating in five previous Olympics and securing multiple other medals.
    - Multiple Olympic Medals: His collection includes a silver medal (2000 Sydney) and bronze medals (2004 Athens, 2008 Beijing).
    - World Championship Silver Medal: While the gold eluded him, a silver at the 2002 World Championship is a testament to his consistent excellence.
    - European Champion: He secured this title in 2013, adding another prestigious trophy to his collection.
    - Club Level Success: With Belogorie Belgorod, Sergey won numerous Russian Championships and Champions League titles.

IMPACT ON THE SPORT:

- Sergey's longevity, consistency, and technical prowess have inspired countless aspiring volleyball players.
- He's known for his sportsmanship and leadership, becoming a true ambassador for the sport in Russia and worldwide.
- After retiring from the national team, Sergey transitioned to a management role at Belogorie Belgorod, ensuring his knowledge and passion continue to shape future generations.

BEYOND THE COURT:

- Known for his calm demeanor and focus on the court, Sergey enjoys a quieter life outside of volleyball.
- He values spending time with his family and remains actively involved in the sport he cherishes.
- Fun Fact: Sergey is a highly decorated athlete, receiving awards like the Order of Honour and Order of Friendship from the Russian government, recognizing his exceptional contributions to volleyball.

INSPIRATIONAL QUOTE:

"Volleyball is a marathon, not a sprint. It takes dedication, hard work, and a love for the game to succeed over the long term." - Sergey Tetyukhin

# Hugo Conte (Argentina)

EARLY LIFE AND INSPIRATION:

- Born in Buenos Aires, Argentina in 1963, Hugo Conte's volleyball journey began at a young age.
- Surrounded by a family passionate about sports, Hugo discovered volleyball through his father, who was a coach.
- He was naturally athletic and drawn to the strategic and fast-paced nature of the sport.

TRAINING AND DEDICATION:

- Hugo dedicated himself to mastering all aspects of the game. He wasn't the tallest player, but his exceptional jumping ability, powerful hitting, and strategic thinking made him a force to be reckoned with.
- He faced challenges early on, playing in a time when Argentina wasn't a dominant force in volleyball. This only fueled his determination to excel.

CAREER HIGHLIGHTS AND ACHIEVEMENTS:

- Hugo became a symbol of Argentinian volleyball pride, leading his country to new heights:
    - Olympic Bronze Medal: Argentina's historic bronze medal win at the 1988 Seoul Olympics was a defining moment, showcasing Hugo's leadership and the team's fighting spirit.
    - World Championship Medalist: He secured a bronze medal at the 1982 World Championship, another significant achievement for Argentinian volleyball.
    - Club Level Success: Hugo played for prestigious clubs in Argentina and Italy throughout his career, winning numerous national and European championships.

IMPACT ON THE SPORT:

- Hugo's charisma, leadership, and all-around skills inspired a generation of Argentinian volleyball players.
- He's considered one of the most intelligent and well-rounded players Argentina has ever produced, elevating the sport's profile in his country.

- After retiring from playing, Hugo transitioned into coaching, sharing his knowledge and passion with aspiring athletes.

BEYOND THE COURT:

- Known for his competitive spirit and tactical mind on the court, Hugo is also admired for his infectious enthusiasm and sportsmanship.
- He enjoys spending time with his family, cycling, and staying involved in the sport he cherishes.
- Fun Fact: Hugo has two sons, Facundo and Mateo, who have also become successful volleyball players, carrying on the Conte legacy.

INSPIRATIONAL QUOTE:

"Volleyball is more than just winning. It's about teamwork, strategy, and leaving everything you have on the court. It's about inspiring others to chase their dreams." - Hugo Conte

Zhu Ting
(China)

Zhu Ting is a true superstar in the world of volleyball, captivating audiences with her exceptional skills and leadership on the court.

EARLY LIFE AND VOLLEYBALL BEGINNINGS (1994-PRESENT):

- Born: November 29, 1994, Dancheng County, Zhoukou, China
- Began playing volleyball at a young age, showcasing her natural talent and athleticism.
- Identified as a promising player early on and entered a prestigious sports school to further develop her skills.

DOMINATING CAREER (2013-PRESENT):

- Position: Outside Hitter (known for her powerful spikes and offensive prowess)
- National Team (China):
    - Olympic Gold Medal: 2016 Rio de Janeiro (First Chinese captain to win Olympic gold in volleyball)
    - FIVB Volleyball World Cup: Silver Medal (2015)
    - FIVB Volleyball Nations League: Gold Medal (2018)
    - Numerous other medals at Asian Games and other international tournaments.
    - Considered a key player in China's recent volleyball success.
- Club Career:
    - Played for prestigious clubs in China and other countries:
        - Henan Huawei (China)
        - Vakıfbank Istanbul (Turkey)
        - Savino del Bene Scandicci (Italy) (Current Club as of May 2024)
    - Won numerous championships at the club level, including the CEV Champions League.

- Playing Style: A dominant force on the court, renowned for her powerful attacks, exceptional jumping ability, and strategic thinking.
- Leadership: Has emerged as a vocal leader on the Chinese National Team, inspiring her teammates with her work ethic and dedication.

OVERCOMING CHALLENGES:

- Zhu Ting has faced challenges throughout her career, including injuries.
- In 2020, she took a break from the Chinese National Team to recover from an injury.
- However, her dedication to the sport and her return to the national team in 2023 demonstrate her unwavering passion for volleyball.

LEGACY AND IMPACT:

- Zhu Ting is widely regarded as one of the greatest volleyball players of her generation.
- Her achievements and playing style have inspired countless aspiring athletes, particularly young girls, in China and around the world.
- She is a global ambassador for volleyball, promoting the sport's growth and popularity.
- She is known for her humility, work ethic, and dedication to her sport and family.

Zhu Ting's exceptional talent, leadership qualities, and dedication to volleyball have solidified her place as a legend in the sport. She continues to inspire future generations and is a true icon of volleyball.

Toomas Sammelvuo
(Finland)
16

EARLY LIFE AND INSPIRATION:

- Born in Pudasjärvi, Finland in 1976, Toomas Sammelvuo's volleyball journey began at a young age.
- Growing up in a sports-loving family, he initially played various sports, but volleyball stole his heart.
- Inspired by his older brother, who was also a volleyball player, Toomas dedicated himself to mastering the outside hitter position.

TRAINING AND DEDICATION:

- With a relentless work ethic, Toomas honed his skills in hitting, jumping, and serving.
- He wasn't the tallest player, but he compensated with an incredible vertical leap and a powerful arm swing, earning him the nickname "The Terminator" for his ability to spike the ball with devastating force.
- Despite facing challenges playing for a smaller volleyball nation like Finland, Toomas's determination to excel never wavered.

CAREER HIGHLIGHTS AND ACHIEVEMENTS:

- Toomas became a symbol of Finnish volleyball pride, achieving success on both the national and international stage:
    - Only Finnish Male Player to Win the Champions League: He secured this prestigious title with Italian club Sisley Treviso in 2006, a historic feat for Finnish volleyball.
    - Long-standing Finnish National Team Member: Toomas represented Finland for over 15 years, leading them to numerous international victories and inspiring a new generation of players.
    - Club Level Success: In addition to the Champions League win, Toomas won numerous championships with clubs across Europe, including Italy, Russia, and Greece.

IMPACT ON THE SPORT:

- Toomas's powerful hitting and international success proved that dominance in volleyball wasn't limited to traditional powerhouses.
- He became an inspiration for aspiring volleyball players in Finland and smaller nations, demonstrating that hard work and dedication can lead to success on the world stage.
- After retiring from playing, Toomas transitioned into coaching, sharing his knowledge and experience with young athletes, including becoming head coach for the Canada National Team.

BEYOND THE COURT:

- Known for his fierce competitive spirit and powerful presence on the court, Toomas is also admired for his positive attitude and leadership qualities.
- He enjoys spending time with his family, outdoor activities like fishing and skiing, and staying involved in the sport he loves.
- Fun Fact: Toomas is a national hero in Finland, and his achievements are a source of immense pride for the country. He has also received prestigious awards like the Finnish Sportsman of the Year.

INSPIRATIONAL QUOTE:

"Volleyball is a game of power, but also of strategy and teamwork. Never give up on your dreams, no matter how big or small your country may be. Believe in yourself, train hard, and anything is possible." - Toomas Sammelvuo

# Earvin Ngapeth (France)

Earvin Ngapeth is a French professional volleyball player who has established himself as one of the most exciting and skilled athletes in the sport today. Here's a breakdown of his impressive career:

EARLY LIFE AND VOLLEYBALL BEGINNINGS (1991-PRESENT):

- Born: February 12, 1991, Saint-Raphaël, France
- Height: 1.94 m (6 ft 4 in)
- Began playing volleyball at a young age, showcasing his talent early on.
- Won gold medals at the U18 and U20 European Championships with the French youth teams.

NATIONAL TEAM SUCCESS (2010-PRESENT):

- A cornerstone of the French Men's National Volleyball Team since 2010.
- Key player in the team's achievements:
    - Olympic Gold Medal at the 2020 Tokyo Olympics, a crowning moment in his career.
    - Gold Medal at the 2015 FIVB Volleyball World League.
    - Silver Medal at the 2012 FIVB Volleyball World League.
    - Numerous other medals at European Championships and World Cups.
- Renowned for his:
    - Powerful hitting and exceptional jumping ability
    - Unpredictable and creative playing style, often making highlight-reel plays.
    - Leadership qualities, inspiring his teammates on and off the court.

Club Career (2008-Present):

- Played for various professional clubs across Europe and Asia throughout his career.

- Won numerous championships and individual awards, including:
  - French League Champion (2010)
  - Italian League Champion (2016)
  - Most Valuable Player awards in various tournaments.
- Currently plays for Halkbank Ankara in the Turkish Volleyball League (as of May 20, 2024).

PLAYING STYLE AND RECOGNITION:

- Often referred to as a "showman" or "magician" for his ability to pull off unexpected and acrobatic plays.
- Though his unorthodox style sometimes leads to errors, his overall impact on the game remains undeniable.
- Earvin Ngapeth is a fan favorite known for his charisma and exciting approach to volleyball.

Earvin Ngapeth's exceptional athleticism, creative playing style, and leadership have made him a global volleyball icon. He continues to inspire fans and aspiring players worldwide with his passion and dedication to the sport.

# Gabi Guimarães (Brazil)

Gabriela "Gabi" Guimarães is a rising star and a key player on the Brazilian Women's National Volleyball Team.

EARLY LIFE AND VOLLEYBALL BEGINNINGS (1994-PRESENT):

- Born: May 19, 1994, Belo Horizonte, Minas Gerais, Brazil
- Height: 1.80 meters (5 ft 11 in)
- Began playing volleyball at the age of 14, initially experimenting with various sports like tennis, football, and swimming.
- Quickly developed a passion for volleyball and displayed exceptional talent.

CLUB CAREER HIGHLIGHTS (2013-PRESENT):

- Played for prestigious Brazilian clubs throughout her career, honing her skills and winning several championships:
    - Itambé/Minas (2013-2018): Won Brazilian Superliga (2018-2019) and South American Club Championship (2019)
    - Rio de Janeiro Vôlei Clube (2018-2021): Won Brazilian Superliga (2018-2019, 2020-2021) and South American Club Championship (2015, 2016, 2017)
    - VakıfBank Spor Kulübü (Turkey, 2021-Present): Won Turkish Women's Volleyball League (2021-2022, 2022-2023), CEV Women's Champions League (2022, 2023), and FIVB Volleyball Women's Club World Championship (2021)

NATIONAL TEAM SUCCESS (2013-PRESENT):

- A vital member of the Brazilian National Team since 2013.
- Contributed significantly to the team's achievements:
    - Olympic Silver Medal at the Tokyo 2020 Olympics
    - Silver Medal at the 2022 FIVB Volleyball World Championship
    - Numerous medals at South American Volleyball Championships, Grand Prix/Volleyball Nations League tournaments.
- Known for her powerful outside hitting, athleticism, and strategic play on the court.

PLAYING STYLE AND FAN FAVORITE:

- Renowned for her explosive attacks, jumping ability, and impressive court coverage.
- Her energetic personality and passion for the game have made her a fan favorite in Brazil and internationally.

BEYOND VOLLEYBALL :

- Maintains a relatively private social media presence compared to some athletes.

Gabi Guimarães is a young and talented volleyball player who has already achieved significant success at the club and national team levels. Her dedication, athleticism, and powerful playing style position her as a future legend in Brazilian volleyball and a role model for aspiring athletes.

Wilfredo León
(Poland)

Wilfredo León Venero is a Cuban-Polish professional volleyball player, renowned for his exceptional skills and powerful presence on the court.

EARLY LIFE AND VOLLEYBALL BEGINNINGS:

- Born on July 31, 1993, in Santiago de Cuba, Cuba.
- Wilfredo's volleyball journey started young. His mother, Alina Venero Boza, was a volleyball player, likely influencing his passion for the sport.
- He displayed exceptional talent at a young age, making his debut with the Cuban national senior team at the remarkable age of 14.

INTERNATIONAL CAREER:

- Cuba (2007-2012): León was a member of the Cuban national team, achieving success:
    - Silver Medal: 2010 FIVB Volleyball Men's World Championship
    - Two-Time Champion: NORCECA Championship (2009, 2011)
- Poland (2019-Present): After receiving Polish citizenship in 2015, León switched allegiance and began representing Poland:
    - Bronze Medal: 2019 CEV European Volleyball Championship
    - Runner-Up: 2019 FIVB Volleyball Men's World Cup

CLUB CAREER:

- León has played for prestigious clubs worldwide, showcasing his talent in various leagues:
    - Sir Safety Perugia (Italy, 2018-2024) - Most recent club
    - Zenit Kazan (Russia, 2014-2018)
    - Al Rayyan S.C. (Qatar, 2015-2016)
    - Earlier stints in Cuban clubs

Playing Style and Recognition:

- León is a dominant outside hitter, known for his powerful spikes, impressive vertical jump, and exceptional athleticism.

- He has garnered comparisons to Cristiano Ronaldo for his superstar status, impact on the sport, and impressive physical prowess.
- Four-time CEV Champions League winner and two-time Most Valuable Player awardee.

BEYOND VOLLEYBALL:

- León found love in Poland and married Małgorzata Gronkowska in 2016.
- They have a daughter, Natalia, born in 2017.

AN INSPIRATION:

- León's journey from his Cuban roots to becoming a Polish standout inspires fans worldwide.
- His dedication, talent, and passion for the sport make him a role model for aspiring volleyball players.

# Tijana Bošković (Serbia)

Tijana Bosković: Serbia's Dominant Force on the Volleyball Court

DOMINATING PRESENCE (1997-PRESENT):

- Born: March 8, 1997, Trebinje, Republika Srpska, Bosnia and Herzegovina
- Height: 1.94 meters (6 ft 4 in)
- Plays the opposite hitter position, known for her powerful attacks, strategic game sense, and exceptional jumping ability.

NATIONAL TEAM TRIUMPHS (2014-PRESENT):

- A cornerstone of the Serbian Women's National Volleyball Team since her teenage years.
- Led Serbia to numerous victories, including:
    - Gold Medals at the World Championships (2018, 2022)
    - Gold Medals at the European Championships (2017, 2019)
    - Bronze Medal at the Tokyo 2020 Olympics

CLUB CAREER ACCOLADES (2015-PRESENT):

- Played for prestigious clubs worldwide, showcasing her talent in:
    - Serbia
    - Turkey
    - China
    - Currently with Eczacıbaşı VitrA (Turkey) as of May, 2024
- Won the 2023 FIVB Volleyball Women's Club World Championship with Eczacıbaşı VitrA, solidifying her dominance at the club level.

NICKNAMES AND RECOGNITION:

- Nicknamed "The Boss" for her leadership qualities and commanding presence on the court.
- Considered one of the greatest opposite hitters of her generation, earning numerous individual accolades like "Most Valuable Player" at various tournaments.

BEYOND VOLLEYBALL :

- Multilingual, speaking Serbian, Turkish, and English.

INSPIRATIONAL QUALITIES:

- Her dedication, work ethic, and perseverance have inspired young volleyball players, particularly in Serbia.
- Her journey from a small town to becoming a global star exemplifies the power of hard work and passion for the sport.

Ivan Zaytsev
(Italy)

Ivan Zaytsev, nicknamed "lo Zar" (the Tsar), is a dominant force on the volleyball court.

EARLY LIFE AND VOLLEYBALL BEGINNINGS:

- Born on October 2, 1988, in Spoleto, Italy, to Russian volleyball parents.
- His' father, Vyacheslav Zaytsev, was an Olympic champion, likely influencing Ivan's early interest in the sport.
- He obtained Italian citizenship in 2008.

PLAYING CAREER AND ACHIEVEMENTS:

- National Team (Italy): Captain of the Italian men's national volleyball team.
- Accolades:
  - Bronze Medal: 2012 Summer Olympics
  - Silver Medal: 2016 Summer Olympics
  - Silver Medal: European Championship (2011, 2013)
  - Bronze Medal: World League (2013, 2014)
  - Italian Champion: 2014
- Club Career: Played for prestigious clubs across Europe and Asia, showcasing his talent in various leagues. Some notable teams include:
  - Sir Safety Umbria Volley (Italy) - Current club
  - Lube Civitanova (Italy)
  - Dynamo Moscow (Russia)
  - Al-Arabi SC (Qatar)
  - Modena Volley (Italy)
- Playing Style and Recognition:
  - Known for his powerful attacks, exceptional jumping ability, and strategic mind on the court.
  - Awarded "Best Server" at the 2013 European Championship and "Best Opposite Spiker" at the 2015 European Championship.

BEYOND VOLLEYBALL:

- Married to Ashling Sirocchi in 2013 and they have a son, Alexander Zaytsev.

IMPACT ON VOLLEYBALL:

- Zaytsev's charisma, leadership, and electrifying playing style have inspired a generation of volleyball players.
- He is a vital part of the Italian national team and a respected competitor internationally.

# Mckenzie Adams (USA)

McKenzie Adams: A Rising Star in American Volleyball

A VERSATILE MIDDLE BLOCKER (1992-PRESENT):

- Born: February 13, 1992, Schertz, Texas, USA
- Height: 1.92 meters (6 ft 3 in)
- Plays the middle blocker position, known for her strong all-around game, including powerful hitting, effective blocking, and strategic awareness.

COLLEGE STANDOUT (2009-2012):

- Played for the University of Virginia and the University of Texas at San Antonio (UTSA).
- Became the first All-American in UTSA program history with an honorable mention in 2012.

NATIONAL TEAM SUCCESS (2019-PRESENT):

- A member of the US Women's National Volleyball Team since 2019.
- Contributed to the team's victory at the 2019 FIVB Volleyball World Cup, showcasing her defensive prowess and offensive capabilities.

CLUB CAREER HIGHLIGHTS (2013-PRESENT):

- Played professionally for various clubs, gaining experience in diverse leagues:
    - Germany
    - Puerto Rico
    - Italy
    - Currently plays for Division 1 team Hisamitsu Springs in Japan (as of May, 2024)

PLAYING STYLE AND FUTURE POTENTIAL:

- Known for her ability to read the game, anticipate opponent's attacks, and deliver impactful blocks.

- Her strong offensive skills add another dimension to her game, making her a valuable asset at the net.
- Considered a rising star with the potential to become a mainstay on the US National Team for years to come.

McKenzie Adams' dedication, well-rounded skillset, and strategic approach to the game have propelled her to success. She is an inspiration for aspiring middle blockers, demonstrating the importance of a strong work ethic and the ability to excel on both offense and defense. As she continues to gain experience, McKenzie Adams is poised to be a leading figure in American volleyball for years to come.

# Leandro Vissotto Neves (Brazil)

Leandro Vissotto Neves is a well-decorated Brazilian volleyball player who has achieved success at both the club and national team levels.

PLAYING CAREER HIGHLIGHTS:

- Born: April 30, 1983 (Rio de Janeiro, Brazil)
- Playing Position: Opposite Hitter
- Height: 2.14 meters (7 ft 0 in)
- Clubs: Played for numerous prestigious clubs in Brazil, Italy, and other countries throughout his extensive career, including:
    - Unisul (Brazil)
    - Flamengo (Brazil)
    - Minas (Brazil)
    - Suzano (Brazil)
    - Latina (Italy)
    - Taranto (Italy)
    - Trentino (Italy) (Two-time Champions League winner)
    - Volei Renata (Brazil)
    - Currently plays for Minas Tênis Clube (Brazil)
- National Team: Represented Brazil at various international competitions:
    - Gold Medal: 2010 FIVB Volleyball Men's World Championship
    - Gold Medal: 2009 FIVB Volleyball Men's World League
    - Gold Medal: 2010 FIVB Volleyball Men's World League
    - Gold Medal: 2009 South American Championship
    - Silver Medal: 2008 Italian League
    - Silver Medal: 2009 Italian League
    - Other Accolades: Won numerous titles at the club level, including Brazilian national championships, Italian Cups, and Club World Championships.

PLAYING STYLE:

- Known for his powerful attacks, impressive reach due to his height, and strategic blocking skills.

CURRENT STATUS:

- As of May 2024, Leandro Vissotto Neves continues his playing career with Minas Tênis Clube in Brazil.

# Isabelle Haak (Sweden)

Isabelle Haak (Sweden)

A DOMINANT FORCE ON THE COURT (1999-PRESENT):

- Born: July 11, 1999, Perstorp, Sweden
- Height: 1.94 meters (6 ft 4 in)
- Plays the opposite hitter position, renowned for her powerful attacks, exceptional jumping ability, and strategic game sense.

NATIONAL TEAM SUCCESS (2014-PRESENT):

- A vital member of the Swedish Women's National Volleyball Team since the young age of 14, becoming the youngest ever player to represent Sweden at the senior level.
- Won the U19 NEVZA (North European Volleyball Zonal Association) Championships in 2014 and 2015 while playing for the Swedish U19 teams.
- Although Sweden hasn't reached the podium at major tournaments yet, Haak's presence inspires hope for future success.

CLUB CAREER ACCOMPLISHMENTS (2016-PRESENT):

- Gained valuable experience playing for prestigious clubs in various countries:
    - Engelholms VS (Sweden, 2012-2016)
    - Béziers Volley (France, 2016-2017)
    - Savino Del Bene Scandicci (Italy, 2017-2019)
    - VakıfBank S.K. (Turkey, 2019-2022) - Won the CEV Women's Champions League (2022)
    - Currently playing for Imoco Volley Conegliano (Italy) as of May, 2024

PLAYING STYLE AND RECOGNITION:

- Known for her powerful spikes, impressive vertical jump, and ability to score from various angles on the court.

- Considered one of the most promising young talents in international volleyball, with many experts predicting even greater achievements in the future.
- Earned the nickname "The Phoenix" for her ability to rise above challenges and consistently deliver strong performances.

Isabelle Haak's exceptional talent, dedication, and work ethic have already secured her place as a rising star in the world of volleyball. Her powerful attacks and strategic play on the court make her a valuable asset to any team. With her young age and continued development, Isabelle Haak has the potential to become a legend in the sport, inspiring future generations of Swedish volleyball players.

# David Lee (USA)

EARLY LIFE AND VOLLEYBALL BEGINNINGS:

- Born: March 8, 1982, in Alpine, California, USA. His talent and passion for the sport blossomed at a young age.

NATIONAL TEAM CAREER (USA):

- A cornerstone of the U.S. Men's National Volleyball Team since 2008.
    - Accolades:Gold Medal: 2008 Summer Olympics (Beijing)
    - Bronze Medal: 2016 Summer Olympics (Rio de Janeiro)
    - Bronze Medal: 2018 FIVB Volleyball Men's World Championship
    - Gold Medal: 2014 FIVB Volleyball Men's World League
    - Gold Medal: 2015 FIVB Volleyball Men's World Cup
    - Numerous other international tournament medals

CLUB CAREER:

- Played for prestigious clubs worldwide, showcasing his talent in various leagues. Some notable teams include:
    - Ziraat Bankası Ankara (Turkey) - Current club (as of May 2024)
    - Zenit Kazan (Russia)
    - Hyundai Skywalkers (South Korea)
    - Perugia Volley (Italy)
    - Pallavolo Modena (Italy)

PLAYING STYLE AND RECOGNITION:

- Renowned for his exceptional hitting power, earning him the nickname "Mattress."
- A highly skilled outside hitter known for his consistency, strategic playmaking, and clutch performances.
- Six-time USAV Male Indoor Player of the Year (2012-2015, 2018-2019)

IMPACT ON VOLLEYBALL:

- David Lee serves as a role model for aspiring volleyball players, inspiring them with his dedication, work ethic, and exceptional skills.
- He is a prominent figure in American volleyball and a respected competitor on the international stage.

Yuji Nishida
(Japan)

Yuji Nishida is a young and exciting talent in Japanese men's volleyball. Here's a breakdown of his impressive career so far:

EARLY LIFE AND CAREER BEGINNINGS (2000-PRESENT):

- Born: January 30, 2000, in Mie, Japan
- Began playing volleyball at a young age, showcasing his potential early on.

CLUB CAREER:

- Played for JTEKT Stings (2017-2021, 2023) in the V.League (Japan's top volleyball league).
- Briefly played for Volley Callipo (Italy) in 2021-2022.
- Currently plays for Panasonic Panthers (2023-Present) in the V.League.

NATIONAL TEAM CAREER (2018-PRESENT):

- One of the youngest players on the 2018 Japanese national volleyball team.
- Key Achievements:
    - Played a pivotal role in securing Japan's first win in 11 years against Italy in the 2018 FIVB Volleyball Men's Nations League, scoring 24 points.
    - Became the youngest player ever to score 30 points in a match at the 2018 FIVB Volleyball Men's World Championship against Argentina.
    - Continues to be a vital member of the national team, contributing significantly to their performance in various international competitions.

PLAYING STYLE:

- Renowned for his impressive left-handed spike, earning him nicknames like "Monster of the Vertical Jump" and "The Terminator."
- Known for his powerful attacks, athleticism, and on-court determination.

IMPACT ON VOLLEYBALL:

- Yuji Nishida is a fan favorite in Japan and a rising star in international volleyball.
- His talent and achievements inspire young players and contribute to the growing popularity of volleyball in Japan.

RECENT CONTROVERSY (JANUARY 2023):

- Nishida faced criticism and suspension from his club for a social media post deemed offensive.

LOOKING AHEAD:

- Yuji Nishida has the potential to become a legendary figure in Japanese volleyball. His dedication, talent, and experience will likely lead him to even greater achievements in the future.

# Fernanda Venturini (Brazil)

Fernanda Venturini is a retired Brazilian volleyball player widely regarded as one of the best setters of all time. Her exceptional skills and leadership on the court have earned her a place among volleyball's royalty.

EARLY LIFE AND VOLLEYBALL BEGINNINGS (1970-PRESENT):

- Born: October 24, 1970, Araraquara, São Paulo, Brazil
- Began playing volleyball at a young age, starting at 11 years old on medical advice to correct scoliosis.
- Demonstrated exceptional talent and dedication to the sport.

DOMINATING PLAYING CAREER (1984-2004):

- Position: Setter (known for her strategic ball distribution and playmaking abilities)
- National Team (Brazil):
    - Won a bronze medal at the 1996 Olympic Games in Atlanta.
    - A key player in Brazil's rise to prominence in women's volleyball.
    - Played alongside other legendary Brazilian players like Ana Moser and Sheilla Castro.
    - Competed in numerous international tournaments throughout her career.
- Club Career: Played for prestigious clubs in Brazil and other countries, achieving numerous titles.

AWARDS AND RECOGNITION:

- 1995 FIVB Volleyball World Cup Champion: A significant achievement in her career.
- Only Brazilian athlete named among the top four greatest women's volleyball players of the 20th century by the FIVB in 2000: A testament to her exceptional talent and impact on the sport.
- Inducted into the International Volleyball Hall of Fame in 2022: A well-deserved recognition for her outstanding career.

PLAYING STYLE AND LEGACY:

- Renowned for her exceptional court vision, strategic setting skills, and leadership qualities.
- Credited with elevating the level of play for her teammates and the Brazilian National Team.
- Considered a role model for aspiring setters, particularly young girls, demonstrating the importance of strategic thinking and teamwork in volleyball.

Fernanda Venturini's exceptional talent, dedication, and leadership have solidified her place as a volleyball legend. Her contributions to the sport continue to inspire future generations of players, especially setters.

# Bartosz Kurek (Poland)

Bartosz Kurek is a Polish volleyball player widely regarded as one of the best outside hitters in the world. Renowned for his exceptional attacking prowess, strategic game sense, and charismatic presence on the court, Kurek has amassed a remarkable collection of accolades throughout his illustrious career.

EARLY LIFE AND VOLLEYBALL BEGINNINGS (1988-PRESENT):

- Born: August 29, 1988, Walbrzych, Poland
- Height: 2.05 meters (6 ft 8 in)
- Began playing volleyball at a young age, following in the footsteps of his father, Adam Kurek, a former Polish national team player.
- Developed his skills through various youth clubs and honed his talent at the prestigious SMS PZPS Szczyrk volleyball school.

NATIONAL TEAM TRIUMPHS (2007-PRESENT):

- A cornerstone of the Polish Men's National Volleyball Team since 2007.
- Led the team to numerous victories, including:
  - Gold Medal at the 2018 FIVB Volleyball World Championship
  - Silver Medal at the 2016 Rio Olympics
  - Bronze Medal at the 2020 Tokyo Olympics
  - Numerous medals at European Championships and other international tournaments.
- Known for his powerful spikes, deceptive shots, and ability to score from anywhere on the court.

CLUB CAREER ACCOMPLISHMENTS (2008-PRESENT):

- Played professionally for prestigious clubs worldwide, showcasing his talent in:
  - Poland
  - Italy
  - Japan
  - Currently playing for Arkas Spor (Turkey) as of May, 2024

- Won numerous domestic league titles and individual awards throughout his career.

PLAYING STYLE AND RECOGNITION:

- Renowned for his exceptional jumping ability, powerful spikes, and ability to read the game strategically.
- Considered one of the most dominant outside hitters of his generation, earning numerous individual accolades like "Most Valuable Player" at various tournaments.
- Nicknamed "Golden Boy" for his impact on Polish volleyball and his captivating playing style.

BEYOND VOLLEYBALL :

- Married to model Zuzanna Mirecka.
- Known for his outgoing personality, fashion sense, and involvement in charitable endeavors.

Bartosz Kurek's exceptional talent, dedication, and charisma have solidified his place as a volleyball legend. He continues to inspire aspiring athletes, particularly young outside hitters, demonstrating the importance of hard work, strategic thinking, and a passion for the sport. Kurek's legacy extends beyond the court, as he has become a cultural icon and a role model for many in Poland and worldwide.

# Lang ping (China)

Lang Ping, also known by her nickname "Iron Hammer," is a true volleyball legend. Her remarkable career encompasses both playing and coaching, solidifying her place as one of the most influential figures in the sport's history. She married Wang Yucheng in 2016.

PLAYING CAREER (1978-1986, 1990):

- Dominant Outside Hitter: A powerful and strategic outside hitter, Lang Ping led the Chinese National Women's Team to numerous victories during her playing career.
- Accolades:
  - Gold Medal: 1984 Summer Olympics (Los Angeles)
  - Gold Medal: 1981 FIVB Volleyball Women's World Cup
  - Gold Medal: 1982 FIVB Volleyball World Championship
  - Silver Medal: 1990 FIVB Volleyball World Championship
  - MVP Award: 1984 Summer Olympics
  - Numerous other awards and accolades throughout her playing career

COACHING CAREER (1995-PRESENT):

  - Coaching Greatness: Following her playing career, Lang Ping transitioned into coaching with remarkable success.
  - Coached multiple national teams, including China and the United States.
  - Accolades:
    - Gold Medal: 2016 Summer Olympics (Rio de Janeiro) with China (First person to win gold as both a player and coach)
    - Bronze Medal: 1995 FIVB Volleyball Women's World Cup with China
    - Silver Medal: 1996 Summer Olympics (Atlanta) with China
    - Silver Medal: 1998 FIVB Volleyball World Championship with China
    - Numerous other coaching achievements at various levels

IMPACT ON VOLLEYBALL:

- Lang Ping's influence on volleyball is undeniable. She has inspired generations of players and coaches through her dedication, tactical brilliance, and unwavering passion for the sport.
- Her coaching style emphasizes discipline, teamwork, and strategic thinking, empowering her teams to achieve peak performance.

INSPIRATIONAL QUOTE (ATTRIBUTED TO LANG PING):

"The road to success is never smooth, but with hard work, perseverance, and a strong team, anything is possible."

LEGACY:

Lang Ping's legacy extends far beyond her impressive list of achievements. She is a role model for athletes and coaches worldwide, a symbol of dedication, and a testament to the power of resilience on the path to greatness.

# Saeid Marouf (Iran)

Saeid Marouf Lakerani, often referred to as the "Wizard" for his exceptional setting skills, is a retired Iranian volleyball player who captivated audiences with his strategic playmaking and leadership on the court.

EARLY LIFE AND VOLLEYBALL BEGINNINGS (1985-PRESENT):

- Born: October 20, 1985, Urmia, West Azerbaijan, Iran
- Height: 1.90 meters (6 ft 3 in)
- Developed a passion for volleyball at a young age, following in the footsteps of his uncles who were also volleyball players.
- Began his career playing for local clubs in his hometown, including Ermia Makavamat.

NATIONAL TEAM SUCCESS (2005-2021):

- A dominant force on the Iranian National Team from 2005 to 2021.
- Instrumental in the team's rise to international prominence, leading them to:
  - Silver Medal at the 2014 Asian Games
  - Numerous medals at Asian Championships and other international tournaments.
  - Captained the team at the 2016 Rio Olympics and 2020 Tokyo Olympics.
- Renowned for his exceptional setting skills, court vision, and ability to orchestrate effective attacks for his teammates.
- Earned numerous individual accolades, including "Best Setter" at the 2014 World League and several Olympic qualification tournaments.

CLUB CAREER HIGHLIGHTS (2005-2021):

- Played for various clubs within the Iranian Volleyball Super League throughout his career, showcasing his talent with teams like:
  - Sanam Tehran
  - Cali Mazandaran
  - Paykan Tehran
  - And others

- Won multiple Iranian Super League championships with different clubs.

LEADERSHIP AND RETIREMENT (2011-2021):

- Briefly stepped away from the National Team in 2011 due to disagreements with management but returned in 2012.
- Became a respected leader and mentor on the team, inspiring younger players with his dedication and experience.
- Announced his retirement from international volleyball in 2021 after the Iranian team's performance at the Tokyo Olympics.

LEGACY AND INSPIRATION:

- Saeid Marouf's exceptional skills and strategic approach to the game redefined the setter position in Iranian volleyball.
- He is considered a legend in Iran and is admired by aspiring volleyball players for his leadership and dedication to the sport.
- While retired from international competition, Marouf's impact on Iranian volleyball continues to inspire future generations of setters.

Saeid Marouf's influence on Iranian volleyball extends beyond his impressive playing career. His nickname, "The Wizard," aptly captures his magical ability to orchestrate plays and elevate his teammates' performance. Marouf's legacy as a leader and a true setter legend continues to inspire players both in Iran and around the world.

Georg Grozer
(Germany)

Georg Grozer, also known as György Grozer, is a German professional volleyball player of Hungarian origin who has carved a remarkable career path. Here's a breakdown of his achievements:

EARLY LIFE AND VOLLEYBALL BEGINNINGS (1984-PRESENT):

- Born: November 27, 1984, Budapest, Hungary
- Married to Violetta Grozer.
- Height: 2.01 meters (6 ft 7 in)
- Began playing volleyball at a young age in Hungary.
- Moved to Germany with his family and continued his volleyball development there.

NATIONAL TEAM SUCCESS (2011-PRESENT):

- A key member of the German Men's National Volleyball Team since 2011 (except for a brief period due to injury).
- Played a pivotal role in the team's achievements, including:
    - Gold Medal at the 2017 European Championship
    - Numerous other medals at European Championships and World League/Volleyball Nations League tournaments.
- Known for his consistent play, powerful attacks, and leadership qualities on the court.

CLUB CAREER ACCOMPLISHMENTS (2000-PRESENT):

- Played professionally for prestigious clubs across Europe and Asia, showcasing his talent in:
    - Hungary
    - Germany
    - Poland
    - Italy
    - South Korea
    - Currently playing for Arkas Spor (Turkey) as of May, 2024

PLAYING STYLE AND RECOGNITION:

- Renowned for his powerful outside hitting, strategic game sense, and ability to adapt to different playing styles.
- Considered a veteran leader who motivates and inspires his teammates.
- Earned numerous individual accolades throughout his career, including "Most Valuable Player" awards at various tournaments.
- Nicknamed "Ice Man" for his calm demeanor and composure on the court.

Georg Grozer's dedication, consistency, and leadership have made him a legend in German volleyball. He continues to inspire aspiring players, particularly young outside hitters, demonstrating the importance of hard work, adaptability, and a strategic approach to the game. With his extensive experience and ongoing competitive spirit, Grozer remains a valuable asset to any team he plays for.

# Kerri Walsh Jennings (USA)

Kerri Walsh Jennings is a household name in beach volleyball, renowned for her exceptional skill, fierce competitiveness, and Olympic glory.

EARLY LIFE AND VOLLEYBALL BEGINNINGS (1978-PRESENT):

- Born: August 16, 1978, Santa Clara, California, USA
- Married to Casey Jennings in 2005.
- Grew up in an athletic family, inheriting her passion for volleyball from her mother, a college standout.
- Excelled in indoor volleyball at Stanford University, winning consecutive NCAA championships (1996 & 1997).

TRANSITION TO BEACH VOLLEYBALL (2000S):

- Began her professional beach volleyball career in the early 2000s, quickly establishing herself as a rising star.
- Partnered with Misty May-Treanor, forming one of the most dominant beach volleyball duos in history.

DOMINANT PARTNERSHIP WITH MISTY MAY-TREANOR (2001-2009, 2011-2012):

- Three Olympic Gold Medals: 2004 Athens, 2008 Beijing, 2012 London
- One Olympic Bronze Medal: 2016 Rio de Janeiro (with April Ross)
- FIVB World Tour Domination: Won 112 consecutive matches and numerous World Tour titles.
- Playing Style: A force to be reckoned with, known for her powerful serving, strategic blocking, and mental toughness.

POST-MAY-TREANOR CAREER (2013-PRESENT):

- Partnered with various talented players like April Ross, Nicole Branagh, and Brooke Sweat.
- Continued to achieve success, winning numerous AVP and international tournaments.
- Secured a bronze medal at the 2016 Olympics with April Ross.

LEGACY AND IMPACT:

- Kerri Walsh Jennings is widely considered one of the greatest beach volleyball players of all time.
- An inspiration for aspiring athletes, particularly young girls, demonstrating dedication, perseverance, and excellence in a traditionally male-dominated sport.
- Holds the record for most career victories (135) in beach volleyball as of 2016.
- Serves as a commentator and advocate for beach volleyball, promoting the sport's growth and popularity.

INSPIRATIONAL QUOTE (ATTRIBUTED TO KERRI WALSH JENNINGS):
"Success is not about winning all the time, it's about never giving up on your dreams."

Kerri Walsh Jennings' contribution to beach volleyball is immeasurable. Her talent, determination, and Olympic achievements have cemented her status as a legend. She continues to inspire future generations and is a true ambassador for the sport.

# Dmitry Muserskiy (Russia)

Dmitry Muserskiy is a Russian volleyball player of Ukrainian descent, renowned for his exceptional height, powerful blocking, and offensive capabilities.

EARLY LIFE AND VOLLEYBALL BEGINNINGS (1988-PRESENT):

- Born: October 29, 1988, Makiivka, Soviet Union (present-day Ukraine)
- Height: 2.18 meters (7 ft 2 in)
- Began playing volleyball at a young age in Ukraine.
- Gained Russian citizenship in 2006.

NATIONAL TEAM TRIUMPHS (2010-PRESENT):

- A vital member of the Russian Men's National Volleyball Team since 2010.
- Instrumental in the team's achievements, including:
  - Gold Medal at the 2012 London Olympics
  - Gold Medal at the 2014 FIVB Volleyball World Championship
  - Numerous medals at European Championships and World League/Volleyball Nations League tournaments.
- Known for his exceptional blocking skills, strategic positioning at the net, and powerful spikes when playing opposite hitter.

CLUB CAREER ACCOMPLISHMENTS (2005-PRESENT):

- Played professionally for prestigious clubs worldwide, showcasing his dominance in:
  - Ukraine (early career)
  - Russia
  - Japan (currently)
  - Won numerous national league titles with Belgorod (Russia)
  - Won the 2014 FIVB Volleyball Men's Club World Championship with Belgorod
  - Currently playing for Suntory Sunbirds (Japan) as of May, 2024

UNIQUE TRAITS AND RECOGNITION:

- One of the tallest athletes in professional volleyball, earning nicknames like "Small boy" (with a touch of irony) due to his friendly personality.
- Considered one of the most dominant middle blockers and opposite hitters of his generation, with exceptional attacking and defensive skills.
- Earned numerous individual accolades throughout his career, including "Best Middle Blocker" and "Most Valuable Player" at various tournaments.

RECENT CONTROVERSY (2022):

- Faced a nine-month suspension from professional volleyball in 2022 due to a positive doping test.

Despite the recent controversy, Dmitry Muserskiy's exceptional talent and achievements on the court solidify his place as a legend in Russian volleyball. His height, combined with his strategic play and offensive capabilities, has made him a force to be reckoned with throughout his career. While his future career path might be uncertain due to the doping suspension, Muserskiy's impact on the sport remains undeniable.

# Inna Ryskal (USSR)

Inna Ryskal was a dominant force in women's volleyball during the 1960s and early 1970s, playing a key role in the Soviet Union's sustained success on the international stage.

EARLY LIFE AND VOLLEYBALL BEGINNINGS:

- Born: June 15, 1944, Baku, Azerbaijan SSR (present-day Azerbaijan)
- Volleyball's popularity in the USSR during her youth likely sparked her passion for the sport.

DOMINATING PLAYING CAREER (1962-1976):

- Position: Universal player (capable of playing various positions)
    - National Team (USSR):
    - Won four consecutive Olympic medals:
        - Silver Medal: 1964 Summer Olympics (Tokyo)
        - Gold Medal: 1968 Summer Olympics (Mexico City)
        - Gold Medal: 1972 Summer Olympics (Munich)
        - Silver Medal: 1976 Summer Olympics (Montreal)
        - Other Accolades:Won the gold medal at the 1970 FIVB Volleyball Women's World Championship.
        - Won gold medals at the European Championships in 1963, 1967, and 1971.
        - Renowned for her athleticism, versatility, and strategic understanding of the game.

IMPACT ON VOLLEYBALL:

- Inna Ryskal's contributions significantly impacted the Soviet Union's dominance in women's volleyball during her era.
- Her skills and leadership qualities undoubtedly inspired future generations of players.

HONORS AND RECOGNITION:

- Awarded the titles of Master of Sports in 1962, Master of Sports of International Class in 1965, and Honored Master of Sports in 1968 by the USSR.
- Received the Medal for Labor Valor and the Order of the Red Banner of Labor by the USSR

LEGACY:

Inna Ryskal's remarkable career played a vital role in solidifying the Soviet Union's position as a volleyball powerhouse. Her achievements as a player and her dedication to the sport continue to inspire aspiring athletes worldwide.

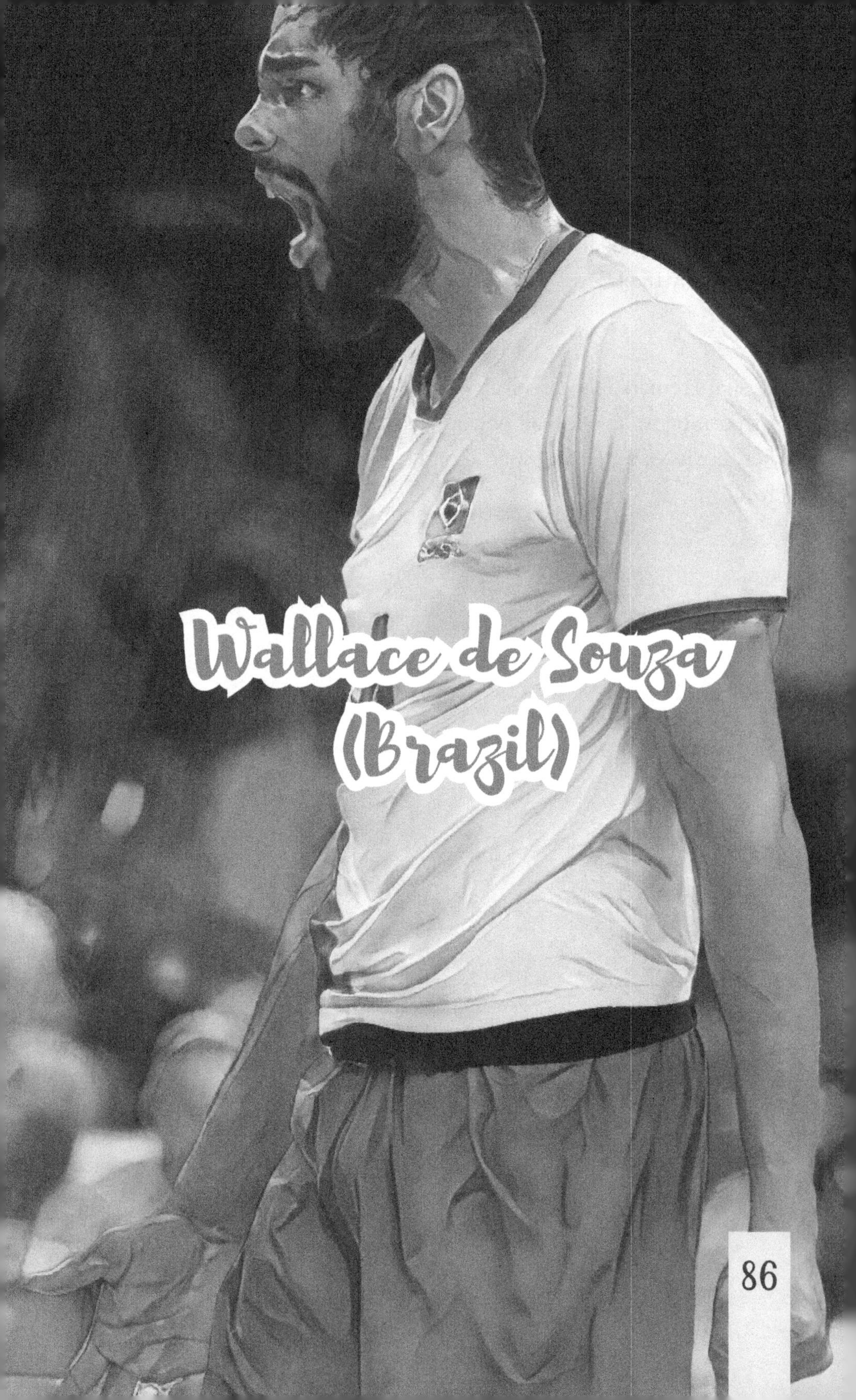

# Wallace de Souza
# (Brazil)

Wallace Leandro de Souza, often known by just Wallace, is a Brazilian volleyball player with a remarkable career overshadowed by recent controversy.

ACCOLADES AND ACHIEVEMENTS:

- Olympic Champion: 2016 Rio Olympics (Brazil Men's Volleyball Team)
- Silver Medalist: 2012 London Olympics
- Three-time South American Champion: 2011, 2013, 2017
- Multiple World Championship and World League medals: Highlighting a long and successful career with the Brazilian national team
- Playing Style: Recognized for his exceptional opposite hitter skills, contributing significantly to the Brazilian team's victories.

RECENT CONTROVERSY:

- In January 2023, Wallace sparked outrage by posting a social media poll. The poll featured a photo of himself holding a shotgun and a question asking his followers if they would "shoot Lula in the face with this 12 [shotgun]?"
- Lula refers to Luiz Inácio Lula da Silva, the newly elected president of Brazil at the time.
- This post caused widespread condemnation due to its violent nature and its targeting of a political figure.
- Wallace faced consequences, including suspension from his club and criticism from the Brazilian volleyball federation.

# Misty May-Treanor (USA)

Misty May-Treanor, also known as Misty May after her marriage, is a legendary figure in beach volleyball. Her dominance on the sand alongside Kerri Walsh Jennings and her individual talent solidify her place among volleyball royalty.

EARLY LIFE AND VOLLEYBALL BEGINNINGS (1977-PRESENT):

- Born: July 30, 1977, Los Angeles, California, USA
- Played volleyball throughout her youth, showcasing her athleticism and passion for the sport.
- Excelled in indoor volleyball at Long Beach State University, winning an NCAA championship in 1998.

TRANSITION TO BEACH VOLLEYBALL (EARLY 2000S):

- Began her professional beach volleyball career in the early 2000s, quickly establishing herself as a rising star.
- Partnered with Kerri Walsh Jennings in 2001, forming a legendary duo that would dominate the sport for over a decade.

UNMATCHED PARTNERSHIP WITH KERRI WALSH JENNINGS (2001-2009, 2011-2012):

- Three Olympic Gold Medals: 2004 Athens, 2008 Beijing, 2012 London
- FIVB World Tour Domination: Won a record-breaking 112 consecutive matches and numerous World Tour titles.
- Playing Style: A versatile player known for her exceptional defensive skills, strategic blocking, and mental fortitude.
- Complementary Skills: The partnership between May-Treanor and Walsh Jennings was a masterclass in teamwork, with their contrasting styles creating an unstoppable force.

Post-Playing Career (2012-Present):

- Briefly retired after the 2012 Olympics, exploring other ventures

- Remained involved in volleyball through coaching and promotional activities.
- May-Treanor served as the Director of Volleyball Operations at Long Beach City College from 2016 to 2020.

LEGACY AND IMPACT:

- Misty May-Treanor is considered one of the greatest beach volleyball players ever.
- An inspiration for young athletes, particularly girls, demonstrating excellence in a traditionally male-dominated sport.
- Holds numerous records, including most career beach volleyball victories (135 as of 2016) when partnered with Walsh Jennings.
- Continues to be an ambassador for volleyball, promoting the sport's growth and popularity.

BEYOND VOLLEYBALL :

- Married Matt Treanor (baseball player) in 2004.
- Known for her dedication to family, her infectious positivity, and her commitment to giving back to the sport.

INSPIRATIONAL QUOTE (ATTRIBUTED TO MISTY MAY-TREANOR):
"Volleyball is more than a game. It's about teamwork, dedication, and pushing yourself to achieve greatness on the sand."

Misty May-Treanor's achievements on the beach volleyball court are legendary. Her skills, partnership with Kerri Walsh Jennings, and her passion for the sport have cemented her place in volleyball history. She continues to inspire future generations and is a true icon of the sport.

Sheilla Castro
(Brazil)

Sheilla Castro, also known by her full name Sheilla Tavares de Castro, is a retired Brazilian volleyball player who achieved immense success on both the national team and club levels.

EARLY LIFE AND VOLLEYBALL BEGINNINGS (1983-PRESENT):

- Born: July 1, 1983, Belo Horizonte, Brazil
- Began playing volleyball at a young age, showcasing her talent and dedication to the sport.

DOMINATING PLAYING CAREER (2001-2022):

- Position: Opposite Hitter
- National Team (Brazil):
  - Two Olympic Gold Medals: 2008 Beijing, 2012 London
  - One Olympic Bronze Medal: 2016 Rio de Janeiro
  - FIVB Volleyball World Grand Prix: Gold Medals (2006, 2009) and numerous other podium finishes
  - South American Championships: Multiple gold medals
- Renowned for her powerful attacks, strategic blocking, and impressive jumping ability.
- Club Career: Played for prestigious clubs in Brazil, Italy, and other countries, winning numerous titles:
  - Brazilian Superliga: Champion with Molico/Osasco and other teams
  - CEV Champions League: Champion with Scavolini Pesaro (Italy)
  - Club World Championship: Champion with Osasco

AWARDS AND RECOGNITION:

- Most Valuable Player (MVP): Awarded the MVP title at various competitions, including the 2006 FIVB World Grand Prix and the 2011 Pan-American Cup.

RETIREMENT AND LEGACY (2022-PRESENT):

- Announced her retirement from professional volleyball in April 2022.
- Sheilla Castro's dedication, exceptional skills, and leadership on the court were instrumental in Brazil's dominance in women's volleyball.
- She continues to inspire young athletes and serves as a role model for aspiring volleyball players worldwide.

Andrea Giani (Italy)

Andrea Giani is a name synonymous with volleyball excellence, both as a player and a coach.

PLAYING CAREER (1988-2005):

- Dominant All-Rounder: Giani was a versatile player, excelling as a middle blocker, outside hitter, and even an opposite spiker throughout his career.
- National Team Hero (Italy): A cornerstone of the Italian national team for 18 years (1988-2005).
    - Accolades:
        - Three Olympic medals (Silver - 1996 & 2004, Bronze - 2000)
        - Three World Championship titles (1990, 1994, 1998)
        - Four European Championships (1993, 1995, 1999, 2003)
        - Seven World League titles (1990-2000) - A record at the time
    - Renowned for his athleticism, powerful attacks, and strategic thinking on the court.

CLUB CAREER:

- Played for prestigious clubs across Europe, showcasing his talent in various leagues:
    - Teams include Sisley Treviso (Italy), Modena Volley (Italy), Power Volley Milano (Italy), Lube Civitanova (Italy), and Friedrichshafen (Germany).

COACHING CAREER (2010-PRESENT):

- Giani transitioned seamlessly into coaching after retirement.
- Coaching Achievements:
    - Head Coach, French Men's National Volleyball Team (Since 2022): Led France to a bronze medal at the 2022 European Championship.
    - Head Coach, Germany Men's National Volleyball Team (2017-2021): Guided Germany to a silver medal at the 2019 European Championship

- Coached various club teams in Italy and Germany, achieving domestic league and cup titles.

PLAYING STYLE AND LEGACY:

- A charismatic leader and a force to be reckoned with on the court, Giani's influence extends beyond his statistics.
- He is admired for his dedication to the sport, his tactical insights, and his ability to inspire players.

BEYOND VOLLEYBALL:

- Personal details about Giani's life beyond volleyball are relatively private.
- He is married to Emanuela Giani and they reportedly have a daughter.

INSPIRATIONAL QUOTE:

"Volleyball is not just a sport, it's a passion. It's about teamwork, strategy, and pushing your limits to achieve greatness." - Andrea Giani

Andrea Giani's journey from a dominant player to a successful coach is a testament to his passion for volleyball and his unwavering commitment to excellence. He continues to inspire athletes and coaches worldwide.

Yumilka Ruiz
(Cuba)

Yumilka Ruiz Luaces, better known as Yumilka Ruiz, is a retired Cuban volleyball player who dominated the sport in the late 1990s and early 2000s. Her exceptional skills and dedication earned her numerous accolades and a place among volleyball's legends.

EARLY LIFE AND VOLLEYBALL BEGINNINGS (1978-PRESENT):

- Born: May 8, 1978, Camagüey, Cuba
- Began training at a Havana sports school at the age of 8, showcasing her athleticism and talent.

NATIONAL TEAM CAREER (1993-2008):

- A cornerstone of the Cuban women's national volleyball team for over a decade.
- Played a key role in establishing Cuba's dominance during her era.
- Accolades:
  - Three Olympic Gold Medals: 1996 Atlanta, 2000 Sydney, 2004 Athens (Team Captain)
  - One Olympic Bronze Medal: 2008 Beijing
  - FIVB Volleyball World Championship: Gold Medal (1998)
  - FIVB Volleyball World Cup: Gold Medal (1999)
  - Numerous other medals at international competitions, including the Pan American Games and NORCECA Championships.

PLAYING STYLE AND LEGACY:

- Renowned for her exceptional attacking skills, particularly her powerful spikes.
- Known for her strategic thinking and ability to elevate her team's performance.
- Considered a complete player with a strong work ethic and leadership qualities.
- Her contributions were instrumental in solidifying Cuba's position as a volleyball powerhouse.

Gilberto Godoy
Filho (Brazil)
BRA

Gilberto Amauri de Godoy Filho, known as Giba, is a retired Brazilian professional volleyball player who played as an outside hitter.

EARLY LIFE AND VOLLEYBALL BEGINNINGS:

- Born on December 23, 1976, in Londrina, Paraná, Brazil.
- Despite severely injuring his left arm in an accident at age 10, Giba's passion for volleyball led him to pursue the sport with determination.

PROFESSIONAL CAREER:

- Giba's professional career spanned over two decades, playing for prestigious clubs in Brazil, Italy, Russia, Argentina, and the United Arab Emirates.
    - Notable Clubs:Ulbra (Brazil)
    - Modena Volley (Italy)
    - Zenit Kazan (Russia)
    - Beşiktaş (Turkey)
    - Al-Rayyan (Qatar)
    - SESC RJ (Brazil)

INTERNATIONAL CAREER (BRAZIL MEN'S NATIONAL VOLLEYBALL TEAM):

- Giba's international career with the Brazilian national team was nothing short of extraordinary.
    - Accolades:Three-time Olympic Gold Medalist: 2004, 2008, 2016
    - World Champion: 2002, 2006, 2008
    - World Cup Champion: 2005, 2007, 2011
    - Eight-time FIVB World League Champion: 2003-2006, 2008-2011
    - South American Champion: 2001, 2003, 2005, 2007, 2009, 2011, 2013, 2015, 2017

PLAYING STYLE AND RECOGNITION:

- Renowned for his exceptional jumping ability, powerful spikes, and strategic playmaking, Giba was a dominant force on the court.
- His charisma, leadership, and electrifying playing style made him a fan favorite and a true icon of the sport.
    - Awards:Best Outside Hitter at the 2008 Olympics
    - FIVB World Player of the Year: 2002, 2006
    - Best Outside Hitter at the 2006 World Championship
    - Best Outside Hitter at the 2003 World Cup

RETIREMENT AND LEGACY:

- Giba retired from professional volleyball in 2017, leaving behind an unparalleled legacy in the sport.
- He is widely regarded as one of the greatest volleyball players of all time, and his impact on the sport continues to inspire generations of athletes.

BEYOND VOLLEYBALL:

- Giba married Maria Luiza Daudt in 2013 and has two sons, Nicoll and Patrick.
- He is involved in various volleyball-related projects, including coaching and promoting the sport.

Giba's exceptional talent, dedication, and passion for volleyball have made him a true legend in the sport. He will forever be remembered as an Olympic icon and an inspiration to aspiring volleyball players worldwide.

Ekaterina Gamova
(Russia)

Ekaterina Aleksandrovna Gamova, also referred to as Yekaterina Gamova, is a retired Russian volleyball player who dominated the sport for over a decade.

A TOWERING PRESENCE ON THE COURT (1980-PRESENT):

- Born: October 17, 1980, Chelyabinsk, Russia
- Nicknamed "The Queen of Volleyball" due to her impressive height (2.02 meters or 6 feet 8 inches) and on-court dominance.
- Retired from professional volleyball in 2016.

NATIONAL TEAM SUCCESS (2000-2016):

- Represented Russia with immense pride, securing numerous accolades:
  - Two Olympic Gold Medals: 2006 (Italy) and 2010 (China)
  - Two Olympic Silver Medals: 2000 (Sydney) and 2012 (London)
  - FIVB Volleyball World Championship Gold Medals: 2006 (Japan) and 2010 (Japan)
  - Numerous other medals at European Championships and other international tournaments.

CLUB CAREER ACCOLADES (1997-2016):

- Played for prestigious clubs in Russia and other countries, achieving remarkable feats:
  - Won the CEV Champions League with Dinamo Kazan in 2014 (held in Baku, Azerbaijan). Named Most Valuable Player (MVP) and Best Scorer of the tournament.
  - Won the FIVB Club World Championship gold medal in 2014, receiving the Best Opposite Spiker and Most Valuable Player (MVP) honors.
  - Claimed numerous other championships at the club level throughout her career.

LEGACY:

- Ekaterina Gamova's influence on volleyball is undeniable.
- Her exceptional skills, leadership qualities, and longevity at the top of the sport have cemented her place among volleyball's legends.
- She continues to inspire future generations with her achievements and dedication to the sport.

Matthew Anderson
(USA)
Modena

Matthew John Anderson is a celebrated American professional volleyball player, widely recognized for his exceptional skills and dedication to the sport.

EARLY LIFE AND VOLLEYBALL BEGINNINGS:

- Born on April 18, 1987, in Buffalo, New York, USA. His talent and passion for the sport blossomed at a young age.

NATIONAL TEAM CAREER (USA):

- A cornerstone of the U.S. Men's National Volleyball Team since 2008.
    - Accolades:Bronze Medal: 2016 Summer Olympics (Rio de Janeiro)
    - Bronze Medal: 2018 FIVB Volleyball Men's World Championship
    - Gold Medal: 2014 FIVB Volleyball Men's World League
    - Gold Medal: 2015 FIVB Volleyball Men's World Cup
    - Numerous other international tournament medals

CLUB CAREER:

- Played for prestigious clubs worldwide, showcasing his talent in various leagues. Some notable teams include:Ziraat Bankası Ankara (Turkey) - Current club (as of May 2024)
- Zenit Kazan (Russia)
- Hyundai Skywalkers (South Korea)
- Perugia Volley (Italy)
- Pallavolo Modena (Italy)

PLAYING STYLE AND RECOGNITION:

- Renowned for his exceptional hitting power, earning him the nickname "Mattress."

- A highly skilled outside hitter known for his consistency, strategic playmaking, and clutch performances.
- Six-time USAV Male Indoor Player of the Year (2012-2015, 2018-2019)

IMPACT ON VOLLEYBALL:

- Matthew Anderson serves as a role model for aspiring volleyball players, inspiring them with his dedication, work ethic, and exceptional skills.
- He is a prominent figure in American volleyball and a respected competitor on the international stage.

Foluke Akinradewo
(USA)
16

Foluke Akinradewo Gunderson is a decorated American indoor volleyball player who has dominated the middle blocker position for both club and national teams.

EARLY LIFE AND VOLLEYBALL BEGINNINGS (1987-PRESENT):

- Born: October 5, 1987, London, Ontario, Canada (holds tri-citizenship with Canada, Nigeria, and the United States)
- Began playing volleyball at a young age, showcasing exceptional talent and athleticism.
- Played high school volleyball at St. Thomas Aquinas High School in Florida.

COLLEGE STARDOM (2004-2008):

- Played for Stanford University, a powerhouse program in collegiate volleyball.
- Won four National Collegiate Athletic Association (NCAA) championships (2005-2008) - a remarkable feat.
- Earned numerous individual accolades:
    - AVCA First-Team All-American (2006-2008)
    - Volleyball Magazine Co-National Player of the Year (2008)

NATIONAL TEAM SUCCESS (2010-PRESENT):

- A key player for the US Women's National Volleyball Team since 2010.
- Secured a gold medal at the 2020 Tokyo Summer Olympics, solidifying her legacy.
- Won silver at the 2012 London Olympics and bronze at the 2016 Rio de Janeiro Olympics, achieving the complete Olympic medal set.
- Numerous medals at FIVB Volleyball World Cups, Nations Leagues, and other international tournaments.

PROFESSIONAL CAREER (2010-PRESENT):

- Played professionally for prestigious clubs worldwide, showcasing her talent in:
    - Japan
    - Italy
    - Turkey
    - Switzerland
    - Currently plays for Hisamitsu Springs in Japan (as of May, 2024)

PLAYING STYLE AND LEGACY:

- Renowned for her exceptional height (6'3"), powerful blocking abilities, and strategic game sense at the net.
- Considered one of the most dominant middle blockers of her generation.
- Her contributions have significantly impacted the US National Team's performance, inspiring future generations.
- A role model for young athletes, demonstrating dedication, hard work, and the ability to overcome challenges.

PERSONAL LIFE:

- Married to Jonathan Gunderson and has a son named Kayode (born 2019).

Foluke Akinradewo Gunderson's exceptional talent, dedication, and perseverance have solidified her place as a volleyball legend. She continues to be an inspiration for aspiring athletes around the world.

# Manon Flier (Netherlands)

Manon Nummerdor-Flier, also known as Manon Flier, is a retired Dutch volleyball player who carved a successful career path as a dominant opposite hitter.

EARLY LIFE AND VOLLEYBALL BEGINNINGS (1984-PRESENT):

- Born: February 8, 1984, Nieuwleusen, Netherlands
- Height: 1.92 meters (6 ft 4 in)
- Developed a passion for volleyball at a young age, playing for local clubs in her hometown.
- Began her professional career at the age of 15, joining the Dutch club Volco Ommen.

NATIONAL TEAM SUCCESS (2003-2015):

- A cornerstone of the Dutch Women's National Volleyball Team from 2003 to 2015.
- Played a vital role in the team's rise to international prominence, contributing to:
    - Silver Medal at the 2018 FIVB Volleyball World Championship (although she wasn't on the active roster for the finals)
    - Numerous other medals at European Championships and other international tournaments.
- Renowned for her powerful attacks, exceptional jumping ability, and strategic game sense on the court.

CLUB CAREER ACCOMPLISHMENTS (2000-2015):

- Played for prestigious clubs across Europe and Asia, showcasing her talent in:
    - Netherlands
    - Italy
    - Turkey
    - China
- Won multiple domestic league titles with various clubs.
    - Notable achievements include:Most Valuable Player at the 2007 FIVB World Grand Prix with the Dutch National Team.

    - Best Spiker award at the 2010–11 CEV Champions League with Scavolini Pesaro (Italy).
    - Bronze Medal with Igtisadchi Baku in the 2013–14 Azerbaijan Super League and the Best Server award.

POST-RETIREMENT (2015-PRESENT):

- Retired from professional volleyball in 2015.

LEGACY AND INSPIRATION:

- Manon Nummerdor-Flier's impressive career has inspired countless young volleyball players, particularly in the Netherlands.
- Her powerful hitting and strategic approach to the game redefined the role of the opposite hitter in Dutch volleyball.
- Even after retirement, Manon Flier remains a respected figure in the volleyball community.

Manon Nummerdor-Flier's dedication, athleticism, and strategic thinking have cemented her place as a Dutch volleyball legend. Her impact on the sport transcends her impressive achievements, as she continues to inspire aspiring players with her legacy of excellence.

# Phil Dalhausser (USA)

Phil Dalhausser is an American former professional beach volleyball player, widely regarded as one of the most dominant athletes in the sport's history. Earning the nickname "The Thin Beast" for his lean physique and ferocious playing style, Dalhausser's career is an impressive display of athleticism, strategy, and unwavering determination.

EARLY LIFE AND VOLLEYBALL BEGINNINGS (1980-PRESENT):

- Born: January 26, 1980, Baden, Switzerland (American citizen)
- Height: 6 ft 9 in (2.06 m)
- Although born in Switzerland, Dalhausser considers Florida his hometown.
- Didn't start playing volleyball competitively until his senior year of high school.
- Played college volleyball for the University of Central Florida, earning a business degree.

OLYMPIC GLORY AND BEACH DOMINATION (2003-2018):

- Partnered with various talented players throughout his career, finding his most successful partnership with Todd Rogers.
- Together, Dalhausser and Rogers achieved remarkable success:
    - Gold Medal at the 2008 Beijing Olympics, with Dalhausser being named tournament MVP.
    - Numerous FIVB World Tour and AVP Tour victories, establishing themselves as a dominant force in beach volleyball.
    - Reached the quarterfinals at the 2012 London Olympics.
- Dalhausser also achieved success with other partners, including Nick Lucena, with whom he competed in the 2016 and 2020 Olympics.

PLAYING STYLE AND ACCOLADES:

- Known for his exceptional blocking skills, strategic positioning at the net, and powerful serving.
- Dalhausser's height provided a significant advantage, allowing him to dominate the net and shut down opposing hitters.

- Earned numerous individual accolades throughout his career, including "Most Outstanding", "Best Blocker", and "MVP" awards in various tournaments.

BEYOND BEACH VOLLEYBALL (PRESENT DAY):

- Retired from professional beach volleyball in 2022.
- Details about his current endeavors are not widely available, but he might be involved in coaching, beach volleyball clinics, or pursuing other business ventures.

LEGACY AND INSPIRATION:

- Phil Dalhausser's relentless work ethic, dedication to the sport, and exceptional skillset have made him a true legend in beach volleyball.
- He is considered a role model for aspiring players, particularly young blockers, demonstrating the importance of strategic thinking, physical dominance, and a competitive spirit.
- Even after retirement, Dalhausser's impact on the sport continues to inspire, with his name synonymous with beach volleyball excellence.

Phil Dalhausser's "Thin Beast" persona captured the essence of his aggressive playing style and relentless pursuit of victory. His dedication and exceptional talent have secured his place as one of the greatest beach volleyball players of all time.

# April Ross (USA)

April Ross is an American beach volleyball player and a three-time Olympic medalist. Renowned for her powerful serve, energetic presence on the court, and unwavering determination, Ross has carved a remarkable career path, inspiring aspiring athletes and captivating audiences worldwide.

EARLY LIFE AND VOLLEYBALL BEGINNINGS (1982-PRESENT):

- Born: June 20, 1982, Costa Mesa, California, USA
- Height: 6 ft 1 in (1.85 m)
- Played volleyball throughout high school, excelling not only in volleyball but also in basketball and soccer.
- Earned a scholarship to play indoor volleyball for the University of Southern California, leading the team to back-to-back NCAA Championships in 2002 and 2003.

BEACH VOLLEYBALL DOMINATION AND OLYMPIC GLORY (2006-PRESENT):

- Transitioned to beach volleyball in 2006, quickly establishing herself as a rising star on the AVP tour (Association of Volleyball Professionals).
- Achieved remarkable success throughout her career, partnering with various talented players:
    - Gold Medal at the 2020 Tokyo Olympics with Alix Klineman, showcasing their exceptional teamwork and dominant presence on the court.
    - Silver Medal at the 2012 London Olympics with Jennifer Kessy, solidifying their position as a top contender.
    - Bronze Medal at the 2016 Rio Olympics with Kerri Walsh Jennings, demonstrating her adaptability and ability to excel with different teammates.
    - Numerous FIVB World Tour and AVP Tour victories with various partners.

PLAYING STYLE AND RECOGNITION:

- Known for her powerful jump serve, a significant weapon that can disrupt opponents' rhythm and create scoring opportunities.
- Possesses excellent defensive skills, strategic awareness, and the ability to deliver impactful attacks.
- Earned numerous individual accolades throughout her career, including "Most Valuable Player" awards in various tournaments.
- Nicknamed "Ross the Boss" for her leadership qualities and dominance on the court.

BEYOND BEACH VOLLEYBALL (LIMITED INFORMATION):

- Married to Bradley Keenan in 2010.
- Known for her outgoing personality, dedication to fitness, and involvement in charitable endeavors.

April Ross's dedication, athleticism, and unwavering determination have propelled her to the pinnacle of beach volleyball. Her three Olympic medals, numerous tour victories, and captivating playing style have cemented her place as an American beach volleyball legend. As she continues to inspire aspiring athletes, April Ross remains a force to be reckoned with on the sand, forever shining as a "Golden Californian."

# Steve Timmons (USA)

Steve Timmons is an American volleyball legend who carved a remarkable career path, excelling in both indoor and beach volleyball. Renowned for his exceptional blocking skills, powerful hitting, and leadership qualities, Timmons' achievements continue to inspire volleyball players worldwide.

EARLY LIFE AND VOLLEYBALL BEGINNINGS (1958-PRESENT):

- Born: November 29, 1958, Manhattan Beach, California, USA
- Height: 6 ft 5 in (1.96 m)
- Developed a passion for volleyball at a young age, playing in his hometown of Manhattan Beach, a hotbed for the sport.
- Played collegiate volleyball at the University of Southern California, honing his skills and laying the foundation for future success.

INDOOR VOLLEYBALL HERO (1984-1992):

- A cornerstone of the United States Men's National Volleyball Team for nearly a decade.
- Instrumental in the team's triumphs, securing:
  - Gold Medal at the 1984 and 1988 Olympics, showcasing his dominance at the highest level.
  - Bronze Medal at the 1992 Olympics, demonstrating his longevity and contribution to the team's success.
  - Numerous other medals at international tournaments like the World Cup and World Championships.
- Recognized for his exceptional blocking skills, strategic positioning at the net, and powerful hitting, earning him the title of "Best Blocker" at the 1988 Olympics.

BEACH VOLLEYBALL SUCCESS (1989-1994):

- While achieving indoor volleyball glory, Timmons also ventured into the beach volleyball scene.
- Partnered with talented players like Karch Kiraly, achieving success in the Association of Volleyball Professionals (AVP) Pro Beach circuit (1989-1994).

- Won a tournament in Enoshima, Japan, with Kiraly in 1989, showcasing his adaptability and talent across both indoor and beach formats.

BEYOND VOLLEYBALL (PRESENT DAY):

- Co-founded Redsand Beachwear, a successful action sports clothing and lifestyle brand, demonstrating his entrepreneurial spirit.
- Currently serves as an assistant coach for the San Diego State University men's volleyball team, sharing his knowledge and experience with future generations of players.

LEGACY AND INSPIRATION:

- Steve Timmons's dedication, athleticism, and leadership have made him a true legend in both indoor and beach volleyball.
- He is considered a role model for aspiring players, demonstrating the importance of hard work, strategic thinking, and a competitive spirit.
- Even after retirement, Timmons remains actively involved in the sport, inspiring and guiding future volleyball stars.

Steve Timmons's achievements transcend mere medals and victories. He has left an undeniable mark on volleyball, not only through his exceptional skills but also through his passion for the sport and dedication to nurturing young talent.

Lloy Ball
(USA)

Lloy Ball is an American former volleyball player who achieved remarkable feats throughout his career. Here's a breakdown of his accomplishments:

EARLY LIFE AND VOLLEYBALL BEGINNINGS (1972-PRESENT):

- Born: February 17, 1972, Fort Wayne, Indiana, USA
- Height: 6 ft 8 in (2.03 m)
- Introduced to volleyball at a young age by his father, Arnie Ball, a volleyball coach.
- Despite the lack of high school volleyball in Indiana, Lloy honed his skills in summer leagues, showcasing his early talent.
- Earned a spot in the 1987 Olympic Festival at the young age of 15, becoming the youngest player to compete in that competition.

NATIONAL TEAM ACCOLADES (1993-2008):

- A vital member of the United States Men's National Volleyball Team for over a decade and a half (1993-2008).
- Played a pivotal role in the team's achievements, including:
    - Gold Medal at the 2008 Beijing Olympics, solidifying his legacy as an Olympic champion.
    - Gold Medal at the 2007 NORCECA Championship and 2008 World League, showcasing his dominance in international tournaments.
    - Numerous other medals at the Pan American Games, World Championships, and World League tournaments.
- Known for his exceptional setting skills, strategic game sense, and leadership qualities on the court.

CLUB CAREER VICTORIES (1991-2012):

- Played professionally for prestigious clubs across Europe and Asia, demonstrating his talent and adaptability:
    - United States (Purdue Fort Wayne)
    - Japan (Toray Arrows)
    - Italy (Casa Modena)
    - Greece (Iraklis Thessaloniki)

    - Russia (Zenit Kazan)
    - Poland (Jastrzębski Węgiel)
    - Turkey (Arkas Spor)
- Won numerous domestic league titles with various clubs throughout his career.

POST-PLAYING CAREER (PRESENT DAY):

- Founded Team Pineapple, a volleyball clinic that offers training opportunities for aspiring players, alongside his father Arnie Ball.
- Details about his other ventures beyond coaching are not widely available online.

LEGACY AND RECOGNITION:

- Lloy Ball's dedication, consistency, and leadership have made him a respected figure in American volleyball.
- He is considered a role model for young setters, especially those following in his footsteps as part of Team Pineapple.
- His "setter attack" innovation has become a trademark, earning him recognition for his contributions to volleyball strategy.
- Inducted into the International Volleyball Hall of Fame in 2015, solidifying his place among volleyball legends.

Lloy Ball's journey from a young prodigy to an Olympic champion and coaching mentor is an inspiration. His exceptional setting skills, strategic leadership, and dedication to the sport have secured his place as a legend in American volleyball.

## Kim Yeon-koung (South Korea)

Kim Yeon-koung: A Volleyball Powerhouse and Inspiration

EARLY LIFE AND INSPIRATION:

- Born in 1988 in Gimcheon, South Korea, Kim Yeon-koung wasn't initially drawn to volleyball.
- Her early athletic passion was basketball, but due to her height (6'2"), a coach recommended she try volleyball.
- This decision sparked a love for the sport, and Kim quickly developed her exceptional skills.

TRAINING AND DEDICATION:

- Kim's rise to stardom wasn't solely based on talent. She is renowned for her relentless work ethic and dedication to training.
- Known for arriving early and staying late to practice extra serves, spikes, and blocking techniques.
- This intense training regimen honed her skills and became a hallmark of her dedication to the sport.

CAREER HIGHLIGHTS AND ACHIEVEMENTS:

- A dominant force on the court, Kim Yeon-koung's career boasts numerous achievements:
  - Olympic Silver Medal: 2012 London Olympics (leading scorer)
  - FIVB Volleyball World Cup Silver Medal: 2015
  - FIVB Volleyball Nations League Gold Medal: 2018
  - Numerous other medals at Asian Games and international tournaments.
  - Recognitions include "Best Outside Hitter" awards and "Most Valuable Player" honors throughout her career.

IMPACT ON THE SPORT:

- Kim Yeon-koung's influence on volleyball extends beyond her impressive trophy cabinet.
- She is considered one of the greatest outside hitters of her generation, inspiring young athletes in South Korea and worldwide.
- Her powerful play and dedication to the sport have helped elevate the profile of women's volleyball.

BEYOND THE COURT:

- Details about Kim Yeon-koung's personal life are relatively private.
- She is known for her humility and dedication to her family.
- There have been rumors of coaching or mentorship roles after retirement, but confirmation is limited.

HERE'S A QUOTE INSPIRED BY HER JOURNEY:

"Success isn't just about talent; it's about the countless hours of practice, the unwavering focus, and the unwavering belief in yourself."

Kim Yeon-koung's story embodies this message, showcasing the power of hard work and passion in achieving greatness.

# Hugh McCutcheon (USA)

Hugh McCutcheon is a former volleyball coach and player who has made significant contributions to the sport in the United States and internationally. Here's a look at his impressive career:

EARLY LIFE AND PLAYING CAREER (1969-PRESENT):

- Born: October 13, 1969, Christchurch, New Zealand
- Gained New Zealand and American citizenship
- Played volleyball competitively during his college years at Brigham Young University (BYU)
- While details about his playing career are not widely available, his transition to coaching suggests a strong understanding of the game.

COACHING SUCCESSES (1995-PRESENT):

- Began his coaching career as a top assistant at BYU under head coach Carl McGown (1995-2001)
- During this time, BYU achieved remarkable success, winning two NCAA Men's Volleyball Championships (1999 and 2001).
- McCutcheon's coaching skills and strategic approach were recognized as instrumental in these victories.

HEAD COACH HIGHLIGHTS (2001-2023):

- Head Coach of the Vienna Hotvolleys in Austria (2001-2003)
- Led the team to win the Austrian League, Austrian Cup, and Inter-Liga championships in his first season.
- Coached the US Men's National Volleyball Team (2006-2008)
- Guided the team to a Silver Medal at the 2008 Beijing Olympics, showcasing his ability to lead at the highest international level.
- Head Coach of the US Women's National Volleyball Team (2009-2012)
- Led the team to consistent success, including a Silver Medal at the 2012 London Olympics.
- University of Minnesota Golden Gophers (2012-2022):
    - This stint marked a significant portion of McCutcheon's career.

- He transformed the Minnesota Golden Gophers Women's Volleyball program into a national powerhouse.
- Achievements include:
  - Three appearances in the NCAA Final Four (2015, 2016, 2019)
  - Two Big Ten Conference Championships (2015, 2018)
  - Coached numerous All-American players, including AVCA and ESPNW National Player of the Year, Sarah Wilhite.

CURRENT ROLE (2023-PRESENT):

- As of January 2023, McCutcheon transitioned to the role of Assistant AD/Sport Development Coach at the University of Minnesota.
- This shift suggests a focus on broader athletic department development and potentially mentoring future coaches.

LEGACY AND RECOGNITION:

- Hugh McCutcheon's coaching career is marked by exceptional achievements and strategic brilliance.
- He is credited with developing winning teams at various levels, from collegiate to international competition.
- Inducted into the International Volleyball Hall of Fame in 2018, a testament to his lasting impact on the sport.

Hugh McCutcheon's dedication to volleyball, strategic coaching approach, and ability to inspire players have earned him a place among volleyball legends. His transition to a broader athletic development role signifies his continued passion for fostering excellence within the sport.

Logan Tom
(USA)

Logan Tom is an American former volleyball player who achieved remarkable success in both indoor and beach volleyball. Renowned for her athleticism, versatility, and leadership qualities, she left an undeniable mark on the sport.

EARLY LIFE AND VOLLEYBALL BEGINNINGS (1981-PRESENT):

- Born: May 25, 1981, Honolulu, Hawaii, USA
- Height: 6 ft 1 in (1.86 m)
- Developed a passion for volleyball at a young age, starting to play competitively at 13.
- Earned a spot on the U.S. Girls' Youth National Team at 14, showcasing her early talent.
- At 16, made her U.S. Women's National Team debut, becoming the youngest woman ever selected for the Olympics at the 2000 Sydney Games.

DOMINATING INDOOR VOLLEYBALL (2000-2012):

- A cornerstone of the U.S. Women's National Volleyball Team for over a decade.
- Played a key role in the team's triumphs, securing:
    - Silver Medal at the 2008 Beijing Olympics, demonstrating her leadership and consistent performance.
    - Numerous other medals at international tournaments like the FIVB World Championship, FIVB World Cup, and FIVB World Grand Prix.
    - Known for her exceptional all-around skills: powerful hitting, strategic serving, and solid defense.
- Earned numerous individual accolades throughout her indoor career, including "Best Outside Hitter" awards in various tournaments.

EXPLORING BEACH VOLLEYBALL (2006-2007):

- Briefly took a break from indoor volleyball to pursue beach volleyball in 2006.

- Partnered with 2009 International Volleyball Hall of Fame inductee Holly McPeak.
- Achieved success, including the title of "2006 AVP Rookie of the Year" and numerous top-10 finishes.
- Ultimately returned to the indoor game in 2007, showcasing her versatility and adaptability.

BEYOND VOLLEYBALL (PRESENT DAY):

- Currently serves as the head coach of the Israel Women's National Volleyball Team, sharing her knowledge and experience with a new generation of players.
- Actively involved in promoting volleyball and inspiring young athletes through various initiatives.

LEGACY AND INSPIRATION:

- Logan Tom's exceptional athleticism, unwavering dedication, and leadership qualities have made her a true legend in volleyball.
- She is considered a role model for aspiring players, particularly young women, demonstrating the power of hard work and versatility.
- Her achievements in both indoor and beach volleyball solidify her place as a well-rounded and dominant force in the sport.

Logan Tom's journey from a young prodigy to an Olympic medalist and coach is an inspiration. Her dedication to volleyball, both as a player and coach, has positively impacted the sport at all levels.

# Reid Priddy (USA)

Reid Priddy is an American volleyball icon who has dominated on both the indoor and beach volleyball courts. His exceptional athleticism, strategic thinking, and relentless drive have earned him a place among the sport's most celebrated players.

EARLY LIFE AND INDOOR VOLLEYBALL BEGINNINGS (1977-PRESENT):

- Born: October 1, 1977, Richmond, Virginia, USA
- Height: 6 ft 4 in (1.94 m)
- Introduced to volleyball in elementary school, quickly igniting a passion for the sport.
- Played competitively throughout high school and excelled at Loyola Marymount University, earning All-American honors.

INDOOR VOLLEYBALL ACCOLADES (1997-2017):

- A dominant force in international indoor volleyball for over two decades.
- Played professionally in prestigious leagues worldwide, including:
  - Greece
  - Russia
  - Turkey
  - Italy
- Contributed significantly to the success of the U.S. Men's National Volleyball Team:
  - Four Olympic appearances (2000, 2004, 2008, 2012)
  - Instrumental in the team's journey, showcasing his leadership and strategic play.
- Earned individual recognition throughout his indoor career, including "Best Scorer" awards in various tournaments.

TRANSITION TO BEACH VOLLEYBALL (2017-PRESENT):

- In 2017, Priddy made a remarkable transition from indoor to beach volleyball, seeking a new challenge.

- Partnered with talented beach players like Trevor Crabb and Taylor Crabb.
- Achieved notable success on the sand:
    - MBBSEA Tour Championship title with Trevor Crabb in 2019
    - Numerous other top finishes, demonstrating his adaptability and continued competitive spirit.
- Aspired to be the second player in history to win gold medals in both indoor and beach volleyball at the Olympics (following Karch Kiraly).

BEYOND VOLLEYBALL (PRESENT DAY):

- Founded the "Max Potential Mindset Course" to share his experiences and inspire athletes to reach their full potential.
- Details about his current endeavors beyond coaching or clinics are not widely available.

LEGACY AND INSPIRATION:

- Reid Priddy's unwavering dedication, exceptional athleticism, and strategic approach to the game have cemented his place as a volleyball legend.
- He serves as an inspiration to aspiring players, demonstrating the power of hard work, adaptability, and a relentless pursuit of excellence.
- His transition to beach volleyball reignited his passion for the sport and showcased his versatility as an athlete.

Reid Priddy's volleyball journey, spanning across indoor and beach courts, is a testament to his enduring passion and exceptional skills. He continues to inspire athletes and contribute to the sport's growth, leaving a lasting legacy as a champion and a role model.

# Megan Hodge (USA)

Megan Hodge (now Megan Hodge Easy) is a decorated American indoor volleyball player who has achieved success at both the collegiate and professional levels. Married former Penn State running back Omar Easy in 2013.

COLLEGE DOMINATION (2006-2009):

- Played for Pennsylvania State University (Penn State) – a powerhouse program in collegiate volleyball.
- Won four consecutive National Collegiate Athletic Association (NCAA) championships (2007-2009) – a remarkable feat.
- Earned numerous individual accolades:
    - Big Ten Player of the Year (2006 & 2009)
    - First-team All-American (2006-2009)
    - NCAA Championship Most Outstanding Player (2007 & 2008)

NATIONAL TEAM CAREER (2010-2012):

- Represented the United States National Team, competing in major international tournaments.
- Secured a silver medal at the 2012 Summer Olympics in London.

PROFESSIONAL CAREER (2010-PRESENT):

- Played professionally for various clubs worldwide, showcasing her talent in:Italy
- Poland
- Azerbaijan
- China
- Most recently, Brazil (as of May 2024) with Minas Tênis Clube

PLAYING STYLE AND LEGACY:

- Renowned for her exceptional height (6'3" or 1.91 meters), powerful hitting and blocking abilities, and strategic game sense.
- Considered one of the most dominant outside hitters of her generation.
- Her contributions helped elevate the US National Team's performance and inspired aspiring athletes.

Sinjin Smith
(USA)

Sinjin Smith, also known by his nickname "The King of the Beach," is an American legend in the world of beach volleyball. Here's a glimpse into his impressive career:

EARLY LIFE AND VOLLEYBALL BEGINNINGS (1957-PRESENT):

- Born: May 7, 1957, Santa Monica, California, USA
- Height: 6 ft 3 in (1.91 m)
- Developed his passion for volleyball at legendary Sorrento Beach in California, learning from pioneers like Ron Von Hagen and Gene Selznick.
- Played collegiate volleyball at UCLA, leading the Bruins to two NCAA Championships (1976 and 1979) and earning All-American honors.

DOMINATING BEACH VOLLEYBALL (1977-2001):

- Began his professional beach volleyball career in 1977, partnering with various talented players.
- Achieved his most significant success with Randy Stoklos, becoming one of the most dominant pairs in men's beach volleyball history.
    - Won an impressive 10 FIVB World Tour titles and 92 AVP Tour victories with Stoklos.
    - Earned recognition as the AVP Best Defensive Player for three consecutive years (1990-1992).
- Smith is credited with being the first player to reach 100 career tournament victories.
- Known for his exceptional defensive skills, strategic positioning, and mental toughness, often employing a one-armed block nicknamed the "Kong Block."

BEYOND BEACH VOLLEYBALL (PRESENT DAY):

- Currently serves on the FIVB Beach Volleyball Commission, overseeing the sport in over 219 member countries, including the Olympics and international games.

- Previously held various leadership roles within volleyball organizations, including President of the AVP and a board member of USA Volleyball.
- Information regarding his current ventures beyond volleyball governing bodies is not widely available.

LEGACY AND RECOGNITION:

- Sinjin Smith's impact on beach volleyball is undeniable. He is considered a pioneer of the sport, inspiring generations of players with his dedication, strategic brilliance, and defensive prowess.
- Inducted into the International Volleyball Hall of Fame, the UCLA Sports Hall of Fame, and his jersey number (22) was retired by UCLA.
- Nicknamed "The King of the Beach," Smith remains a revered figure in the sport, leaving a lasting legacy of dominance and innovation.

Sinjin Smith's journey from a young player honing his skills on Sorrento Beach to becoming a beach volleyball legend and leader in the sport is truly inspiring. His relentless pursuit of excellence and contributions to the game have secured his place in volleyball history.

# Dain Blanton (USA)

Dain Blanton is an American former beach volleyball player who has carved a remarkable career path. Here's a breakdown of his achievements:

EARLY LIFE AND VOLLEYBALL BEGINNINGS (1971-PRESENT):

- Born: November 28, 1971, Laguna Beach, California, USA
- Height: 6 ft 3 in (1.85 m)
- Excelled in both basketball and volleyball at Laguna Beach High School, ultimately choosing volleyball.
- Played collegiate volleyball at Pepperdine University, winning an NCAA Championship in 1992.

BEACH VOLLEYBALL DOMINATION (1997-2010):

- Partnered with various talented players throughout his professional beach volleyball career.
- Achieved significant success, particularly with:
    - Eric Fonoimoana: Won the Gold Medal at the 2000 Sydney Olympics, a defining moment in his career.
    - Jeff Nygaard: Became the first U.S. male beach volleyball player to compete in two Olympic Games (2000 and 2004).
- Won numerous other accolades:
    - Eight AVP Tour victories
    - Numerous podium finishes on the AVP and FIVB tours
    - Earned the distinction of being the first male African-American to win a major beach volleyball event (1997 AVP Hermosa Grand Slam).

PLAYING STYLE AND RECOGNITION (KNOWN FOR):

- Renowned for his athleticism, powerful hitting, and exceptional blocking skills.
- Earned the nickname "Dain the Brain" for his strategic thinking and court awareness.
- Received individual recognition throughout his career, including "Most Outstanding Player" awards in various tournaments.

Beyond Beach Volleyball (Present Day):

- Currently serves as the Head Coach of the University of Southern California's Women's Beach Volleyball program, leading them to back-to-back NCAA Championships (2021 and 2022).
- Works as a sports broadcasting analyst, covering beach volleyball, volleyball, and other sports for various networks like NBC, ABC, and ESPN.
- Remains active in motivational speaking, inspiring young athletes with his story and dedication to the sport.

LEGACY AND INSPIRATION:

- Dain Blanton's Olympic gold medal, combined with his numerous tour victories and coaching success, solidify his place as a beach volleyball legend.
- He is considered a role model for aspiring athletes, particularly young African-Americans in volleyball, demonstrating the power of perseverance and athletic excellence.
- His transition to coaching and broadcasting showcases his continued passion for volleyball and his dedication to sharing his knowledge with future generations.

Dain Blanton's journey from a collegiate standout to an Olympic champion and successful coach is a testament to his dedication and well-rounded skillset. He remains a significant figure in the world of beach volleyball, inspiring athletes and enriching the sport with his knowledge and passion.

# Keba Phipps (USA)

Keba Phipps, also known by her full name Prikeba Reed Phipps, is a retired American volleyball player who left her mark on the sport with an impressive career spanning two Olympics. Here's a closer look at her achievements:

EARLY LIFE AND VOLLEYBALL BEGINNINGS (1969-PRESENT):

- Born: June 30, 1969, Los Angeles, California, USA
- Height: 6 ft 3 in (1.90 m)
- Developed a passion for volleyball at a young age.
- Played volleyball throughout high school and excelled at the collegiate level at the University of Central Florida.

DOMINATING THE NATIONAL TEAM (LATE 1980S-2004):

- Earned a spot on the U.S. Women's National Volleyball Team in the late 1980s.
- Played a vital role in the team's success at various international tournaments:
    - Bronze Medal at the 1987 Pan American Games
    - Silver Medal at the 1987 NORCECA Continental Championship
    - Bronze Medal at the 1989 NORCECA Continental Championship
- Became known for her:
    - Powerful hitting
    - Exceptional blocking skills
    - Strategic court presence

OLYMPIC APPEARANCES (1988 AND 2004):

- The youngest member of the U.S. Women's National Volleyball Team at the 1988 Seoul Olympics, showcasing her talent at a young age.
- Returned to the Olympics in 2004 with a different team, demonstrating her dedication and longevity in the sport.

- While the U.S. team did not medal in either Olympics, Phipps's contributions were significant, particularly in the 1988 games where she played in all five matches.

BEYOND VOLLEYBALL (PRESENT DAY):

- Details about Keba Phipps's current endeavors are not widely available online.
- Some sources suggest she might be involved in coaching or volleyball clinics, but this information is not confirmed.

LEGACY AND RECOGNITION:

- Keba Phipps's achievements include competing in two Olympics, a significant feat in itself.
- Her contributions to the U.S. Women's National Volleyball Team during the late 1980s and early 2000s helped pave the way for future generations of players.
- She is remembered for her exceptional athleticism, strategic play, and dedication to the sport.

Keba Phipps's volleyball career, spanning two decades and two Olympic appearances, is an inspiration for aspiring athletes. Her powerful presence on the court and dedication to the sport have earned her a place in volleyball history.

# Danielle Scott-Arruda (USA)

Danielle Scott-Arruda is an American former volleyball player who holds the record for most Olympic appearances by a female volleyball athlete in the United States. Her remarkable career spanned 19 years, filled with international success and a lasting impact on the sport.

EARLY LIFE AND COLLEGIATE STARDOM (1972-PRESENT):

- Born: October 1, 1972, Baton Rouge, Louisiana, USA
- Height: 6 ft 3 in (1.88 cm)
- Developed a passion for volleyball at a young age.
- Played both volleyball and basketball in high school, becoming the first athlete in the Big West conference to earn all-conference honors in both sports during the same season.
- Excelled at California State University, Long Beach, earning numerous accolades:
  - Three-time AVCA All-American (1991, 1992, 1993)
  - 1994 Honda-Broderick Award winner (now the Honda Sports Award) for the nation's best collegiate female volleyball player
  - Led the NCAA in career hitting efficiency (.421)

DOMINATING THE NATIONAL TEAM (1994-2012):

- A cornerstone of the U.S. Women's National Volleyball Team for nearly two decades (1994-2012).
- Played under five different head coaches and thrived within various team systems, demonstrating her versatility and adaptability.
- Key player in the team's achievements:
  - Silver Medals at the 2008 and 2012 Olympic Games
  - Gold Medals at the 2001 and 2012 FIVB World Grand Prix tournaments
  - Numerous other medals at international tournaments like the FIVB World Cup and FIVB World Championships
- Renowned for her:
  - Powerful hitting and exceptional blocking skills
  - Strategic presence on the court
  - Leadership qualities

BREAKING OLYMPIC RECORDS (1996-2012):

- Competed in a record-breaking five Olympic Games (1996, 2000, 2004, 2008, 2012).
- This achievement stands as a testament to her dedication, longevity, and consistent performance at the highest level.

BEYOND VOLLEYBALL (PRESENT DAY):

- Currently runs Danielle Scott Enterprises, offering volleyball training programs and financial literacy workshops in the Baton Rouge area.
- Remains passionate about volleyball and continues to inspire young athletes.

LEGACY AND RECOGNITION:

- Danielle Scott-Arruda's volleyball journey is an inspiration for aspiring players, particularly young women.
- Her record-breaking number of Olympic appearances, combined with her international medals and collegiate accomplishments, solidify her place as a volleyball legend.
- Inducted into the International Volleyball Hall of Fame in 2018, a prestigious honor recognizing her lasting impact on the sport.

Danielle Scott-Arruda's dedication, athleticism, and leadership have left an undeniable mark on American volleyball. Her record-breaking Olympic appearances and international success continue to inspire athletes to reach their full potential.

# Eric Fonoimoana (USA)

Eric Fonoimoana is an American former beach volleyball player who achieved remarkable success on the sand. He's also known for his philanthropic efforts and current career in real estate. Here's a breakdown of his achievements:

BEACH VOLLEYBALL DOMINATION (1990S-2000S):

- Born: June 7, 1969 (age 54)
- Height: 6 ft 3 in (1.90 m)
- Nicknamed "The Body" for his impressive physique and athleticism
- Partnered with various talented players throughout his career, most notably Dain Blanton.
- Olympic Gold Medal: Won the coveted gold medal at the 2000 Sydney Olympics with partner Dain Blanton, a defining moment in his career.
- Dominant AVP Tour Player: Won at least one tournament for seven straight years (1998-2004), showcasing his consistency and dominance.
- Earned numerous other accolades:
    - AVP Most Valuable Player Award
    - Top 10 in all-time AVP tournaments played
    - Career earnings exceeding $1 million

BEYOND THE BEACH (PRESENT DAY):

- Currently works as a Real Estate Broker Associate in the South Bay area of Los Angeles, California.
- Known for his "Gold Medal Standard" approach to client service, drawing parallels between his work ethic in sports and real estate.

PHILANTHROPY AND COMMUNITY INVOLVEMENT:

- Founded Dig for Kids (D4K), a non-profit organization that helps underserved children excel in academics and volleyball.
- Personally raised over $1 million through D4K, demonstrating his dedication to helping young people.

COACHING AND LEGACY:

- Briefly served as the head coach for his alma mater Mira Costa High School's girls' varsity beach volleyball team, leading them to several championships.
- Owns and operates Elite Beach Volleyball, offering training opportunities for aspiring players.
- Eric Fonoimoana's impact on beach volleyball is undeniable. His Olympic gold medal, combined with his AVP Tour achievements and philanthropic efforts, solidify his place as a legend in the sport.
- He is considered a role model for young athletes, particularly those of Samoan descent, demonstrating the power of hard work and dedication.

Eric Fonoimoana's journey from a beach volleyball champion to a successful real estate professional and philanthropist is an inspiring story. His dedication to excellence and commitment to giving back to the community continue to leave a positive impact.

Thank you for completing your journey through "Legends of Volleyball: 50 Iconic Athletes and the Stories that Defined Them, for Young Readers."

We sincerely hope you have found the reading experience both enlightening and enjoyable.

Our commitment is to consistently deliver high-quality historical literature that engages and educates. We deeply appreciate your dedication to reaching the conclusion of this book.

If you found the content compelling and informative, we kindly request that you consider leaving a review. Your feedback is crucial in helping us maintain our standards and continue to produce exceptional books for our readers.

Thank you once again for your support.

Warm regards,

*Kimmich Prints*

Made in the USA
Monee, IL
09 December 2024